Cambridge Studies in French

FLAUBERT'S CHARACTERS

Cambridge Studies in French

General editor: MALCOLM BOWIE

Also in the series:

J. M. COCKING
Proust. Collected Essays on the Writer and his Art

LEO BERSANI
The Death of Stéphane Mallarmé

MARIAN HOBSON
The Object of Art. The Theory of Illusion in Eighteenth-Century France

RHIANNON GOLDTHORPE
Sartre: Literature and Theory

ANN MOSS
Poetry and Fable. Studies in Mythological Narrative in Sixteenth-Century France

LEO SPITZER
Essays on Seventeenth-Century French Literature
(Translated and edited by David Bellos)

NORMAN BRYSON
Tradition and Desire. From David to Delacroix

ANDREW MARTIN
The Knowledge of Ignorance. From Genesis to Jules Verne

FLAUBERT'S CHARACTERS

THE LANGUAGE OF ILLUSION

DIANA KNIGHT

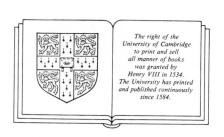

The right of the
University of Cambridge
to print and sell
all manner of books
was granted by
Henry VIII in 1534.
The University has printed
and published continuously
since 1584.

CAMBRIDGE UNIVERSITY PRESS

CAMBRIDGE

LONDON   NEW YORK   NEW ROCHELLE

MELBOURNE   SYDNEY

Published by the Press Syndicate of the University of Cambridge
The Pitt Building, Trumpington Street, Cambridge CB2 1RP
32 East 57th Street, New York, NY 10022, USA
10 Stamford Road, Oakleigh, Melbourne 3166, Australia

© Cambridge University Press 1985

First published 1985

Printed in Great Britain at
the University Press, Cambridge

Library of Congress catalogue card number: 84-23847

British Library Cataloguing in Publication Data
Knight, Diana
Flaubert's characters : the language of illusion.
—(Cambridge studies in French)
1. Flaubert, Gustave—Criticism and interpretation
I. Title
843'.8   PQ2249
ISBN 0 521 30475 X

CONTENTS

Acknowledgements	*page*	vii
Introduction: Character and value		1
1 Oriental aesthetics		7
2 The merits of inarticulacy		25
3 By-passing speech		41
4 Endless illusions		55
5 Overturning reality		74
Conclusion: Making madness more mad		96
Notes		103
References		119
Index		123

ACKNOWLEDGEMENTS

I should like to thank the British Academy (for a grant enabling me to explore the dossier for *L'Éducation sentimentale*), the University of Nottingham (for a period of study leave), and friends and students at Nottingham, Warwick and University College Dublin who have taken an interest in my research. I am especially indebted to Roger Huss, Malcolm Bowie and Jonathan Culler.

GENERAL EDITOR'S PREFACE

This series aims at providing a new forum for the discussion of major critical or scholarly topics within the field of French studies. It differs from most similar-seeming ventures in the degree of freedom which contributing authors are allowed and in the range of subjects covered. For the series is not concerned to promote any single area of academic specialisation or any single theoretical approach. Authors are invited to address themselves to *problems*, and to argue their solutions in whatever terms seem best able to produce an incisive and cogent account of the matter in hand. The search for such terms will sometimes involve the crossing of boundaries between familiar academic disciplines, or the calling of those boundaries into dispute. Most of the studies will be written especially for the series, although from time to time it will also provide new editions of outstanding works which were previously out of print, or originally published in languages other than English or French.

Introduction
CHARACTER AND VALUE

Any study of a past writer is likely to be marked by the critic's own interests, and certainly by his theoretical presuppositions as to the essential areas of interest. Yet strangely, in the case of Flaubert, two contradictory critical approaches, representing opposed attitudes to literature itself, arrive at somewhat similar conclusions. On the one hand, contemporary French sensitivity to Flaubert's modernity leads to an insistence upon the lack of a stable meaning; on the other, a whole Anglo-Saxon tradition finds his novels severely wanting in human interest and moral complexity. Evaluation of Flaubert's status as a major writer is clearly at stake for both sides: the modern critic finds his attention to language and to the formal possibilities of the novel exemplary, while the Leavisite seeker of an appeal to the adult mind cannot honestly appreciate his work at all. The latter is unable to account for the merit which he nevertheless half recognizes in Flaubert;[1] the former, if asked to explain the long-held belief that Flaubert was not just a manic stylist, but equally a representational writer with a world-view to communicate, would doubtless relegate that belief to the realm of ideological prejudice and inferior, naive reading.

The influential view of Flaubert as not only elusive ironist but also supreme dismantler of all stable values and transcendental fixed presences, probably reached its high point at the 1974 Cerisy colloquium on the production of meaning in Flaubert (Gothot-Mersch, 1975). Its chairwoman, a highly respected traditional researcher into Flaubert's intentions,[2] gallantly sums up the mood of the conference with a ruling for 'la faillite de l'illusion représentative': 'C'est donc dans un jeu de déplacement (*décalage, discordance, hiatus, écart, intervalle* ...), dans un glissement perpétuel, que nous avons cherché le sens.' She adds, however, her own timid, but seemingly more seriously felt suggestion, that realism was in fact more important to Flaubert than the participants had implied, that he did not merely construct the deconstruction of meaning, but equally things as solid as

1

bovarysme. Schematizing her dilemma as an obligation to choose between 'reproduction' or 'production' as the best description of Flaubert's method, she equates reproduction with a 'sens plein, idéologique', and production with the constant calling into question, by the 'work' of the language, of any stable meaning at all (pp. 431–4).

To show that this schematic choice is a misleading one is a central concern of my book. For in treating Flaubert as a self-conscious but representational writer, I shall explore the interaction of the illusion of reality and the supposedly more problematic sphere of 'production'. Calling attention to writing as writing and to the methods of literature need not demand the complete loss of illusion, nor the devaluation of 'subject matter'. Jean Ricardou, who treats all novels as battle grounds between the referential and the literal illusions − between what he calls, in a celebrated aphoristic formula, 'the writing of an adventure' and 'the adventure of a writing' (1968, p. 265) − praises Flaubert for insisting methodically upon this opposition, for refusing to reduce the presence of the text by fascinating the reader with events (1971, p. 34). I shall demonstrate, however, that despite Flaubert's important obsession with the material qualities of language, his readers are the object of a double seduction: that he aspires to fascinate them with text and events alike, that *both* are made the focus of an absorbed but self-conscious attention. The combination of both adventures to produce a particular aesthetic impact is achieved as much by the reader's engagement with a particular fiction as by the wallowing in sounds, rhythms and other textual effects that Flaubert encourages as well. The way in which a traditional content therefore relates to Flaubert's general artistic strategy should be distinguished from Ricardou's more radical claim for those novels (the *nouveau roman* and its precursors) which fall clearly into the 'adventure of a writing' camp: that themes and fictions offer a self-conscious dramatization of the novel's own formal concerns, that if fiction does use a vision of the world it does so in order to create a universe obeying the specific laws of writing, and that fictional psychologies and sociologies can thus only return the reader to the functioning of the book (1967, pp. 25–6). For I have no wish to suggest that Flaubert's novels are ultimately 'about' the process of writing. However, it is awareness of that process and its aesthetic purpose that conditions our evaluation of content, that affects the way we read story, theme and character.

Indeed, it is in their evaluation of Flaubert's 'subject matter' that my disagreement with the Anglo-Saxon moral tradition will be found to lie. While modern critics tend to admire Flaubert's supposed lack of content, James, Lawrence, Leavis and Turnell simply despise the content they find. To please the latter, the 'mature' novelist must not only write about life, he must also, unfortunately for Flaubert, like it as well. Flaubert is therefore condemned out of hand for his obvious lack of the 'reverent openness before life' which Leavis attributes to the writers of his Great Tradition (1972, p. 18).[3] Since, as is well known, Flaubert hated existence, himself, and a large proportion of contemporary humanity, he could not be expected to display the enthusiasm for life which subtle moral ramifications apparently demand. But one way in which I aim to reconcile a formalist approach with more traditional moral readings is by exploring the reader's engagement with Flaubert's work precisely on the level of values and evaluations, and by showing that this must take place *within* his awareness of reading as an aesthetic experience. Such awareness must be distinguished from the reader's recognition of the world, for it is undoubtedly its relentless search for such recognition, and a consequent 'relevance to life', that has led the moral tradition to misread Flaubert. A 'correct' moral reading will only be obtained if the joys of lived experience are mediated by the sophistications of formal awareness.

In particular I wish to reinstate the organizing function of *character* as a centre of value. It is striking that the denial of any value system in Flaubert by both moral and structuralist critics depends, in each case, on a particular aesthetic of character. On the one hand character is without doubt the traditional focus for the defence of the novel as a humanizing influence. The belief in the fundamental connection between character and value is stated clearly and typically by E. M. Forster. Whereas a novelist requires curiosity for his plot, he demands 'human feelings and a sense of value for the characters' (1941, p. 141), 'he prefers to tell his story about human beings; he takes over the life by values as well as the life in time' (p. 92). Indeed Henry James focuses his dissatisfaction with Flaubert's 'lack of reach' (1962, p. 211) on his use of mediocre characters as reflectors of experience, dismissing them as a defect of Flaubert's mind — either because they are the best he can manage, or, if not, because he could deliberately create such paltry beings. Banished to the world of 'simpler souls' with no 'finesse' of mind (p. 211), Emma Bovary is pronounced altogether 'too small an affair' (p. 199); of Frédéric Moreau James asks 'why, why him?' (p. 200); Mme Arnoux is condemned as a mistake 'somehow moral', a 'compromising blunder', the worse in that Flaubert does not realize he is committing it: 'We do not pretend

3

to say how he might have shown us Mme Arnoux better – that was his affair. What is ours is that he really felt he was showing her as well as he could, or as she might be shown' (p. 204). That James is wrong about Flaubert's intentions in creating these so-called 'weak vessels' can easily be shown.[4] What matters for the moment is that a particular view of the function of literature prevents him from even contemplating a positive explanation of banal and wilfully unsophisticated characters.

At the other extreme the structuralist dismantling of the individuality and psychological coherence of both the real-life and the fictional self has led to a sustained undermining of the previously assumed central importance of character in literature.[5] Ricardou, certain that the whole notion of character is on the path of decline, claims that Flaubert's use of limited reflectors is a sign of his modernity, a metaphor for the function of character in a modern text. Discussing Flaubert's letter to Sainte-Beuve about *Salammbô*, in which he suggests that the pedestal (the novel) is too big for its statue (Salammbô herself), Ricardou argues that this cannot possibly be an unavoidable fault, but must be Flaubert's subterfuge for saying that character in a novel is no longer comparable to a statue on a pedestal (1971, p. 235).

Jonathan Culler, in his important argument about Flaubert's 'uses of uncertainty', sets out to read the novels through this changed convention:

> Although it is possible to treat *L'Éducation sentimentale* as a study in character, to place Frédéric Moreau at the centre and to infer from the rest of the novel a rich psychological portrait, we are now at least in a position to ask whether this is the best way to proceed. When we approach the novel in this way, we find, as Henry James complained, an absence or emptiness at the centre. The novel does not simply portray a banal personality but shows a marked lack of interest in what we might expect to be the most important questions: what is the precise quality and value of Frédéric's love for Mme Arnoux? for Rosanette? for Mme Dambreuse? What is learned and what is missed in his sentimental education? We can, as readers and critics, supply answers to these questions and this is certainly what traditional models of character enjoin us to do. But if we do so we commit ourselves to naturalizing the text and to ignoring or reducing the strangeness of its gaps and silences.
> (1975, pp. 231–2)

Culler basically agrees with Henry James's assessment of Flaubert's characters, but sees them as one of several ploys for setting up an indeterminate space of uncertainty, for demoralizing the reader by blocking his search for coherence, for challenging the easy construction of meaning. Readers will be defeated by the banality of characters, and will be forced to organize their reading in a different and more sophisticated way.

If I have spelled out the impressive logic of Culler's argument, it is because I shall take issue with it on two grounds. First, as subsequent chapters will show, I cannot agree with the evaluation of Flaubert's characters upon which it depends. Second, as Culler himself has argued elsewhere, structuralist criticism should perhaps investigate as a habit of reading the conviction that 'everything in the novel exists in order to illustrate character and its development', rather than dismissing it as an ideological prejudice (1975, p.230).[6] Roland Barthes contends that while characters should not be made 'psychological' (in the sense of removing them from their paper existence into the real world of possible motives and so on), they should not be wiped out either. For characters are 'des types du discours', produced by the discourse so that it can play with them, rather than let them play with each other (1970, p.184). Character and discourse are accomplices, and to study the construction and characteristics of the former hardly involves assuming that they are 'real people'.[7] And it is surely the case that for the nineteenth-century novel at least 'character' is the novelist's *chief* accomplice. Certainly I am unconvinced that it is a concentration on character as such which severely limits readings of Flaubert,[8] for he appears to work within the convention of character as a major totalizing force in fiction. The Anglo-Saxon tradition's 'mistake' is to ally character to the production of moral, life-relevant values, allowing room for 'form' only through a conception of style as the outer casing for 'content'.

Paradoxically, given that what Henry James says about Flaubert appears to foster this view,[9] his own account of the double role of Maggie Verver in *The Golden Bowl* is perfectly applicable to the relationship between character, composition and value in Flaubert:

the Princess, in fine, in addition to feeling everything she has to, and to playing her part in just that proportion, duplicates, as it were, her value and becomes a compositional resource, and of the finest order, as well as a value intrinsic. So it is that the admirably endowed pair, between them, as I retrace their fortune and my method, point again for me the moral of the endless interest, and endless worth for 'delight', of the compositional contribution. (1981, p.9)

The difference, of course, is that James's compositional resources, even where their field of knowledge is restricted (take the extreme case of *What Maisie Knew*), are subtle reflecting intelligences 'of the finest order'. Clearly what limits James's reading of Flaubert is his search for *intelligent* characters.

5

In taking character as the pivot between formal and moral values in Flaubert, I shall challenge both structuralist devaluations of the general role and status of character in his work, and traditional readings of many of his well-known protagonists. By arguing that the use of unintelligent reflectors of experience is part of a positive intention, I shall show that the very characters dismissed by both the moral and the formalist approaches as 'weak vessels' should be viewed as *exemplary*, since they acquire privileged aesthetic status and are central to the operation of Flaubert's value system. This privilege is won through their special role in relation to essential aspects of Flaubert's aesthetic: the opaqueness of language and experience, stupidity, repetition, fascination and reverie as the aim of art. All of these, I shall go on to claim, are brought about by the behaviour of Flaubert's characters, and in particular by their pathological relationship to both reality and language. It is the latter that renders them supremely complicit in Flaubert's creation of a self-consciously foregrounded illusion of reality, and it is by exploring the links between the content of his fictions and his aesthetic aims and practice, that I hope to refocus interest in Flaubert as a representational writer.

1
ORIENTAL AESTHETICS

A ghostly meeting with a caravan in the Egyptian desert, which makes Flaubert shudder all over with physical pleasure, conveys the intensity of effect that he aspires to create for the readers of his novels:

une caravane nous croise, les hommes entourés de coufiehs (les femmes très voilées) se penchent sur le cou des dromadaires; ils passent tout près de nous, on ne se dit rien, c'est comme des fantômes dans des nuages. Je sens quelque chose comme un sentiment de terreur et d'admiration furieux me couler le long des vertèbres, je ricane nerveusement, je devais être très pâle et je jouissais d'une façon inouïe. Il m'a semblé, pendant que la caravane a passé, que les chameaux ne touchaient pas à terre, qu'ils s'avançaient du poitrail avec un mouvement de bateau, qu'ils étaient supportés là dedans et très élevés au-dessus du sol, comme s'ils eussent marché dans des nuages où ils s'enfonçaient jusqu'au ventre.   (II, p.595)[1]

Jean-Paul Sartre explains the acute enjoyment of this incident by the peculiar manner of apprehending reality which it permits. Flaubert would prefer (and comes to seek) a relationship with reality which puts man and the world similarly out of reach, for there is no contact in this encounter with the real people and animals who slip into a kind of nothingness. In a strange confusion of 'être' and 'apparition' impressions are received as if they were being imagined, and aesthetic joy is generalized from this to embrace any event which reveals experience as a product of the imagination, and which brings about what Sartre calls the 'derealization of the real':

l'être comme apparition, l'apparition réduite à l'apparence, l'essence de la communication se dévoilant comme non-communication absolue, l'imaginaire et le réel confondus, voilà ce qui, tout à coup, fait trembler Flaubert de terreur et de joie. On aura déjà compris que cette joie est celle de l'*esthète*: elle lui est donnée quand les conditions sont réunies pour que l'événement *réalise la déréalisation du réel* et lui montre l'espèce humaine comme un produit de son imagination.   (*L'Idiot* II, p.1564)[2]

7

Flaubert's characters

That Sartre's obsession with the question of why writers become writers should focus finally upon Flaubert, and that he should understand him so well, is certainly because Flaubert offers exemplary illustration of Sartre's early theses on the ontological status of both the artist and the artistic work. His analysis of the meeting with the caravan is an excellent reading of the passage; while the passage itself is a fine example of what Sartre means by the 'point de vue esthétique':

Dire que l'on 'prend' devant la vie une attitude esthétique, c'est confondre constamment le réel et l'imaginaire. Il arrive cependant que nous prenions l'attitude de contemplation esthétique en face d'événements ou d'objets réels. En ce cas chacun peut constater en soi une sorte de recul par rapport à l'objet contemplé qui glisse lui-même dans le néant. C'est que, à partir de ce moment, il n'est plus *perçu*; il fonctionne comme *analogon* de lui-même, c'est-à-dire qu'une image irréelle de ce qu'il est se manifeste pour nous à travers sa présence actuelle.   (1940, p. 245)

This 'aesthetic attitude' is an essential concept for Sartre's early phenomenological descriptions of the activities of the imagination which are so central to his whole ontology and to his thesis on Flaubert. Since my own argument in this book owes some basic assumptions to *L'Idiot de la famille*, I wish to be clear from the outset about what Sartre means (and what I shall mean) by the aesthetic or imaginary attitude.

Every stage of the reasoning in *L'Imaginaire* (1940) could well apply to the case of Flaubert. Sartre starts from a phenomenological description of what imagining is like, and from an initial distinction between perception and imagination as two alternating modes of consciousness, he goes on to pose Kantian questions: what are the characteristics that can be attributed to consciousness from the fact that it is a consciousness capable of imagining? what must its general nature be for the construction of an image always to be possible? He concludes that it must possess the possibility of positing a hypothesis of unreality; that it must be able to escape from the world by its very nature. Imagination is neither some mental source nor some accidental feature of the mind, but is defined as an essential and transcendental condition of consciousness, the whole of consciousness adopting a different mode whereby it realizes its freedom to negate.

As a primary structure of consciousness imagining is still consciousness *of* something (the image is a mental form rather than a simple content of consciousness), but it involves forming objects which possess a trait of nothingness in relation to the whole of reality:

8

une image n'est pas une sensation réveillée, ou remodelée par l'intellect, ni même une ancienne perception altérée ou atténuée par le savoir, mais quelque chose d'entièrement différent, une réalité absente, révélée dans son absence même à travers ce que j'appelais un 'analogon': un objet servant de support analogique et traversé par une intention. (1972, p. 118)

The distinction is between being 'given-as-absent' and being 'grasped-as-nothing', that is 'grasped-as-nothing-*for-me*'. It is because nothing-ness cannot be posited for itself, but only 'lived', that Sartre's complicated analyses are necessary, as in the helpful example of looking at the photograph of Pierre:

Je pense, disions-nous, Pierre dans le tableau. Ceci veut dire que je ne pense pas du tout le tableau; je pense Pierre. Il ne faut donc pas croire que je pense le tableau 'comme image de Pierre'. Ceci est une conscience réflexive qui dévoile la fonction du tableau dans ma conscience présente. Pour cette conscience réflexive, Pierre et le tableau font deux, deux objets distincts. Mais dans l'attitude imageante, ce tableau n'est rien qu'une façon, pour Pierre, de m'apparaître absent. (1940, p. 39)

But the 'attitude imageante' (at work as we remember people and things, as we watch actors, look at paintings, read books), is hard to maintain, and the 'object as image' acquires a discontinuous, jerky character, for it constantly appears and disappears. A long analysis of the experience of watching an impersonation (Franconay 'doing' Maurice Chevalier), clarifies this idea, for Sartre shows that we operate a continual to-and-fro between perception and imagination, between what Franconay is (a small woman wearing a straw hat and making faces), and what she is not (Maurice Chevalier as image). Though overall we may feel this as a mixed, ambiguous condition, we are at any moment free to adopt either attitude (pp. 40–5).

Similar analyses are applied to various aesthetic phenomena, for example looking at a portrait painting of Charles VIII, which involves a similar to-and-fro between 'blobs of paint on a canvas' and 'Charles VIII as image': 'Ainsi le tableau doit être conçu comme une chose matérielle *visitée* de temps à autre (chaque fois que le spectateur prend l'attitude imageante) par un irréel qui est précisément *l'objet peint*' (p. 240). In other words it is not the case that unreal ideas or an image are made real (on canvas, for example), but that real materials (say blobs of paint), are used to produce an imaginary or absent object, and it is in this sense that the aesthetic object is something unreal.

Since, by definition, there is no 'imaginary world', there can be no question of analysing the details of the absent object. What is at stake, as in fiction, is rather a matter of belief. Images remain isolated from each other, for there can be no other relationship between them except the ones consciousness can conceive at each moment in constituting them (p. 215):

> L'objet n'est pas individué: voilà une première raison pour que l'irréel ne se constitue pas en monde. En second lieu, tout objet irréel apportant avec lui son temps et son espace se présente sans aucune solidarité avec aucun autre objet. Il n'est rien que je sois obligé d'accepter en même temps que lui et par lui: il n'a pas de milieu, il est indépendant, isolé − par défaut et non par excès; il n'agit sur rien, rien n'agit sur lui: il est *sans conséquence* au sens fort du terme. (pp. 174−5)

In an exchange of letters with Taine on the difference between the 'artistic hallucination' and a real one, Flaubert describes the former in terms that Sartre might happily have borrowed to explain what he means:

> Dans l'hallucination artistique, le tableau *n'est pas bien limité*, quelque précis qu'il soit. Ainsi je vois *parfaitement* un meuble, une figure, un coin de paysage. Mais cela flotte, cela est suspendu; ça se trouve je ne sais où. Ça existe seul et sans rapport avec le reste, tandis que, dans la réalité, quand je regarde un fauteuil ou un arbre, je vois en même temps les autres meubles de ma chambre, les autres arbres du jardin, ou tout au moins je perçois vaguement qu'ils existent. L'hallucination artistique ne peut porter sur un grand espace, se mouvoir dans un cadre très large. Alors on tombe dans la rêverie, et on revient au calme, c'est même toujours comme cela que cela finit.
>
> Vous me demandez si elle s'emboîte dans la réalité ambiante? non. − La réalité ambiante a disparu. Je ne sais plus ce qu'il y a autour de moi. J'appartiens à cette apparition, exclusivement.
>
> Au contraire, dans l'hallucination pure et simple, on peut très bien voir une image fausse d'un œil, et les objets vrais de l'autre.
>
> (*Corr. Suppl.* II, p. 96 (1866))[3]

The illusion and reality are on two different planes; it is not possible to grasp both at once − Flaubert refers to the 'fleeting' characteristic of the image in a way reminiscent of the to-and-fro involved in maintaining 'Maurice Chevalier as image'.[4]

Sartre himself puts the 'perpetual evasion' of the image in a slightly different perspective by going on to claim that it may seem to offer an escape from present preoccupation and boredom, if not from all worldly constraints. In other words a more radical conception of the imaginary attitude would use it as a negation of the actual condition of 'being-in-the-world' (1940, p. 175), and it is here that the difficult but very interesting question of an *evaluation* of the aesthetic attitude poses itself:[5] 'Tout homme est une fuite de gaz par laquelle il s'échappe dans l'imaginaire. Flaubert était constamment cela' (1972, p. 118). While every perception of the real has the possibility of reversing itself in imagination, which is simply Sartre's definition of the normal transcendental relationship to reality ('néantisation'), it presumably requires a constant return to affirmative existence to valorize it.[6] But when the imaginary attitude is adopted all the time, from preference, it becomes unhealthy, and Sartre devotes a long analysis to the category of individuals who prefer to lead an 'imaginary' life (1940, pp. 189–226). For the schizophrenic adopts imaginary feelings for the sake of their unreal nature, choosing an impoverished, unnatural and formalized life not only as an escape from the content of reality (poverty, failure etc.), but from the very form of reality – the characteristic of 'presence' and the sort of positive reaction it demands of us (p. 189).

Now while it is obviously possible to recognize elements of Flaubert, and certainly of many of his fictional characters, in this psychotic extreme, the imaginary attitude which so easily turns into an unhealthy preference for a particular way of life has been shown to be the normal way of experiencing a work of art. And although Flaubert's own adoption of the unreal as the supreme value is not therefore simply pathological, there is surely some ambiguity in Sartre's argument. For example in establishing the vicious circle of unrealities that he needs to explain the symbiotic relationship between man, work and period in Flaubert's case (the basic thesis of *L'Idiot de la famille*), having distinguished from the outset between the real imaginative consciousness and the unreal object, Sartre explains that there cannot be a causal relationship going from object to consciousness: 'l'irréel ne peut être vu, touché, flairé, qu'irréellement. Réciproquement il ne peut agir que sur un être irréel' (1940, p. 176). To suggest that every experience of an aesthetic object is 'neurotic' is acceptable in the sense that it is in accord with Sartre's definitions; yet it calls into question the supposed malice which Sartre also attributes to the unreal Flaubert who would make the world and his readers unreal through unreal works of art. Not only would Flaubert be intending an inevitable result, but the contagious unreality would be less of a curse than a blessing, if it could impart the extraordinary joy that accompanies the aesthetic attitude in Flaubert's meeting with the phantom-like caravan. This is a problem that my own discussion of the function of supposedly pathological characters will explore. For evaluation of the status of reality in Flaubert's work will reveal an important area in which characters ranging from mildly neurotic to near psychotic could be seen as in some sense privileged – in

11

that an abnormal relationship to reality gives access to the aesthetic realm.

Sartre claims that his greatest problem in constructing the thesis of *L'Idiot de la famille* was to introduce the concept of the imaginary as the cardinal determination of a person (1976, p. 101), and its opening chapters carefully outline the 'constitution' that will lead Flaubert to 'choose himself' as an imaginary being. From his earliest days the infant Flaubert's essential passivity involves hebetude, credulity, a pathological relationship to language and truth, 'comédies' and deliberately upheld beliefs, in all a good apprenticeship in hysteria (*L'Idiot* I, pp. 178).[7] Indeed Flaubert's reaction to his initial conception of himself as an inferior being is to radicalize his maladjustment to reality. His preference for passivity and for the imaginary realm emerges precisely because he secretly believes in the superiority of practical success in the real world.[8] This deliberate reinforcement of his anomaly leads him through various incarnations of imaginary beings – generous 'seigneur', role player, comic actor, author-actor, poet – up to the decisive attempt to unite the contradictions of his own 'lack of reality' with the more positive demands of his family and class. By becoming an 'être-écrivain', Flaubert will consolidate the unreal in literary works.

A clear example of this basic process of self-incarnation as an 'imaginary' being is the discussion of Flaubert's early vocation as actor (*L'Idiot* I, pp. 662–5). Of course this is one of Sartre's favourite stamping-grounds,[9] but there is well-known evidence of Flaubert's early passion for the stage: 'Le fond de ma nature est, quoi qu'on dise, le saltimbanque. J'ai eu dans mon enfance et ma jeunesse un amour effréné des planches. J'aurais été peut-être un grand acteur, si le ciel m'avait fait naître plus pauvre' (*Corr.* (B) I, p. 278 (1846)). In line with the claim that the aesthetic object is something unreal (that real materials are used to produce an imaginary object), Sartre makes his own contribution to the paradox of the actor by putting him forward, like the statue of Venus in an explanatory digression, as a 'centre réel et permanent d'irréalisation' (*L'Idiot* I, p. 786).[10] Diderot is right that the actor does not really feel his character's feelings, but he does not express them 'de sang froid' either (I, pp. 662–3). Rather he feels them in an 'unreal' way; sacrificing himself so that an appearance can exist, he chooses to be a support of non-being. Reducing himself publicly to an exterior appearance, Flaubert becomes an 'analogon' of Harpagon, just as Kean does of Hamlet. Only an imaginary child, says Sartre, could have the idea of guaranteeing in his person the victory of the image over reality, and this heroic nightly self-derealization, to lead the audience into its own collective derealization, is seen partly as the ultimate act of generosity (as are all of Flaubert's roles from the Garçon to Saint-Polycarpe), and partly as the ultimate act of masochism, for Flaubert is introducing into himself the value judgements of the enemy: 'Le défi du petit Gustave est une impuissante provocation en ceci qu'il revendique dans l'orgueil ce qu'il a vécu dans la honte: tu m'as déréalisé? Fort bien, je serai le Seigneur de l'Irréel' (*L'Idiot* I, p. 834). This is especially so in the case of the comic actor, for an analysis of the laugh shows it to have a similar function to the imaginary attitude, since it achieves the derealization of its object by reducing it to pure appearance: to a spectacle without practical consequence.

For Sartre, opting for non-being is the very essence of art, and it is his claim that in order to be an artist around 1850 one *needs* to be neurotic that permits his breathtakingly daring thesis: that Flaubert submits himself to the famous epileptiform illness of 1844 in order to accede to the condition of artist. From Flaubert's point of view, at least, Sartre resolves the ambiguity over evaluation of the aesthetic attitude. For if everyone possesses the faculty of overturning reality, it is only for the artist that it becomes a 'categorical imperative'. Flaubert's 'calling' is to anchor the impossible in the real by tearing himself from the world, by carrying within himself an *exigence* of impossibility, by never deserting the artist's world-view: always to consider reality from the point of view of the unreal. Pride becomes both an ethical and an aesthetic imperative, for pride will give the individual this aesthetic vision (*L'Idiot* II, p. 1566). The points of view of death, the infinite and the absolute all become synonymous with the aesthetic attitude, while Flaubert's famous 'qu'est-ce que le beau sinon l'impossible?' (*Corr.* (B) I, p. 23 (1837)) supports Sartre's definitions of beauty as the dialectical link between being and non-being: 'le réel n'est jamais beau. La beauté est une valeur qui ne saurait s'appliquer qu'à l'imaginaire et qui comporte la néantisation du monde dans sa structure essentielle' (1940, p. 245).

Few critics have wanted or dared to give whole-hearted support to Sartre's extraordinary claims for Flaubert,[11] and there is little discussion of one of the most important of these: that the 1844 fit allowed Flaubert to reinvent the art of writing, to define a literary art involving a radical upheaval in the use of words. For Sartre's final move is to relate the aesthetic attitude to the world to Flaubert's deliberate exploitation of language experienced as an opaque, autonomous order. It is on this crucial connection that Flaubert's conception of art is founded, and on this foundation that my own reading of his fiction has been built.

Sartre's 'Scripta manent' chapter (*L'Idiot* I, pp. 906–78) introduces Flaubert's new fascination with the written word, which is seen to have positive advantages over the spoken one. That the written word should 'remain' is important not for its own sake (immortality or whatever), but because it can be dwelt on at length and tends to force the reader into an attitude of contemplation. It is ultimately preferred as a superior agent of derealization. In the incantatory repetition, described in the early work *Novembre*, of magical words such as 'femme' and 'maîtresse' (I, p. 249), Sartre suggests that the word, as the mediator between the narrator and the mysterious desire, becomes itself the real source of fascination. This is even more apparent in the verbally rich meditation on India and other distant places: 'Oh! l'Inde! l'Inde surtout!' (I, p. 271), 'puissé-je périr en doublant le Cap, mourir de choléra à Calcutta ou de la peste à Constantinople' (I, p. 272). Rather than express the wish, the rich sounds actually satisfy it; indeed false and unlikely desires are created so as to bring the word into being. The true desire is not to live or die in Calcutta, but to trace the letters and to shut himself inside them. While some rudimentary knowledge of the romantic charms of Calcutta is required, the meaning of the sentence will be not so much lost as subsumed. To pass through a word to its meaning is equated by Sartre with perception, whereas to grasp a word in its material singularity is to 'imagine' it. Writing and reading are normally pursued through a subtle dialectic of the two, but to adopt the imaginary attitude to words is to conserve and emphasize their sumptuous materiality (*L'Idiot* I, p. 929). With particularly rich sounds this process happens automatically, but Flaubert makes it happen for all language: the very attitude of derealization forces language to deliver up its materiality (I, p. 931).

Thus what others might prefer to call the foregrounding of the signifier is equated, in a crucial step, with the adoption of the aesthetic attitude to language. This idea is subsumed into the concept of 'style', no longer a gift or an ornament, but simply, for Flaubert, a way of contemplating language. The artist, already required to adopt the aesthetic attitude to the world and to experience, discovers a particular use of language as the essential way of making things imaginary for the reader, which is Sartre's contribution to interpreting the well-known remark by Flaubert that style is a 'manière absolue de voir les choses' (*Corr.* (B) II, p. 31 (1852)). However coherent the discourse, it will be derealized by its formal beauty, for the aesthetic attitude will turn language away from any practical aims: 'les informations sont du domaine des signes mais le *sens* d'un ouvrage de l'esprit nous est communiqué indirectement par sa beauté formelle' (*L'Idiot* II, p.1619). The very meaning of style comes to be the systematic derealization of speech: 'le silence dans le discours, le but imaginaire et secret de la parole écrite' (II, p.1618). The subject matter will be as absent and otherworldly as the caravan in the desert which formed my exotic starting point. Indeed the travel notes and letters from the trip to the Orient illustrate quite specifically the interrelation of the imaginary attitude to the world and to language that I have sought to establish so far. Just as the opaqueness of a strange foreign tongue often acts as a catalyst for the aesthetic attitude to events, so Flaubert will learn to foreground the material qualities of language. This should encourage the readers of his novels to apprehend their represented fictions in an ideal state of avid contemplation.

In an interview given in 1977, Roland Barthes declares:

Quand je voyage, ce qui m'intéresse le plus, ce sont les lambeaux d'art de vivre que je peux saisir au passage. La sensation de plonger dans un monde facile et opaque (pour le touriste, tout est facile). Pas la plongée canaille mais l'immersion voluptueuse dans une langue, par exemple, dont je ne perçois que les sons. C'est une chose qui repose énormément, de ne pas comprendre une langue. Ça élimine toute vulgarité, toute bêtise, toute agression.

(1981, p.249)

For Flaubert, too, it is very much the constant presence of a particularly strange-sounding foreign language which keeps the whole trip to the Orient on the level of an aesthetic experience, of which the chief features — not understanding situations, stupefied contemplation, and reverie — merge constantly into a sort of ecstasy, captured by the familiar 'Ah! tout cela est bien farce' (*Corr.* (B) I, p.553 (1849)).

   Much of the pleasure of sleeping with Arab prostitutes appears to stem from the impossibility of communicating with them: 'ses mots arabes que je ne comprenais pas. C'étaient des questions de trois et de quatre mots et elle attendait la réponse; les yeux entrent les uns dans les autres, l'intensité du regard est doublée. — Mine de Joseph au milieu de tout cela. — Faire l'amour par interprète' (II, p.561). Indeed Flaubert spends a night of 'intensités rêveuses infinies', contemplating the sleeping Ruchiouk-Hânem, and recalling her voice 'qui chantait des chansons sans signification ni mots distinguables pour moi' (*Corr.* (B) I, p.607 (1850)). Ten years later he still misses 'ces amours silencieux où les âmes seules se parlent, ces tendresses sans paroles, ces passivités de bête où se dilate l'orgueil viril' (*Corr.* (C) IV, p.382 (1860)), of which the following ought to have been a prized example: 'J'ai baisé sur une natte d'où s'est déplacée une nichée de chats, étrange coït que ceux où l'on se regarde sans pouvoir parler. Le regard est doublé par la curiosité et l'ébahissement' (*Corr.* (B) I, p. 541 (1849)). From explicit statements of particular delights: 'J'entendais Joseph et les gardes qui causaient à voix basse; je me suis livré là à des intensités nerveuses pleines de réminiscences' (II, pp. 574–5), one infers the intended effect of less stressed passages: 'Je m'endors dans ma pelisse, savourant toutes ces choses; les Arabes chantent un canzone monotone, j'en entends un qui raconte une histoire: voilà la vie du désert' (p. 562). Flaubert frequently inserts strange words into his text:

Couvent Copte. Moines à l'eau descendant tout nus de la montagne: 'Cawadja christiani, batchis, cawadja christiani'; et les échos dans les grottes répètent 'Cawadja, cawadja'. (p. 571)

Femme voilée d'un grand morceau de soie noire toute neuve, et son mari sur un autre âne. 'Taïëb', et l'on répond 'Taïëb, taïëb' sans s'arrêter. (p. 558)

Since he invariably records such words and phrases twice over – 'In ny a oh: in ny a oh!' (p. 586); 'El Kods, el Kods' (p. 607); 'tâe! tâe' (p. 655) – the reader is led to a double perception of the materiality of words: by the rich, unusual sounds, and by their repetition. When Flaubert tries to convey the effect of privileged moments he often resorts to repeating a phrase, as in his account of meeting the caravan: 'ça marche… ça marche…' (p. 596), or of his admiration for camels: 'ça avance, ça avance…' (*Corr.* (B) I, p. 686 (1850)), or of approaching Beirut from the sea: 'on repart, on s'arrête, la lune est couchée, étoiles, étoiles' (II, p. 602).

These special oriental descriptions are characterized by varying degrees of inability to understand and refusal to understand, but all are marked by a lack of thought:[12] 'Je tombe dans des rêveries et des distractions sans fin. – Je suis toujours un peu comme si j'avais trop bu; avec ça, de plus en plus inepte et inapte à comprendre ce qu'on m'explique' (*Corr.* (B) I, p. 678 (1850)). But this blank stupidity is moulded into something more valuable, and Flaubert clearly enjoys his semi-permanent metaphorical inebriation:

Si tu savais quel calme tout autour de nous, et dans quelles profondeurs paisibles on se sent errer l'esprit! Nous paressons, nous flânons, nous rêvassons. (*Corr.* (B) I, p. 588 (1850))

C'est alors que, jouissant de ces choses, au moment où je regardais trois plis de vagues qui se courbaient derrière nous sous le vent, j'ai senti monter au fond de moi un sentiment de bonheur solennel qui allait à la rencontre de ce spectacle, et j'ai remercié Dieu dans mon cœur de m'avoir fait apte à jouir de cette manière; je me sentais fortuné par la pensée, quoiqu'il me semblât pourtant ne penser à rien; c'était une volupté intime de tout mon être.

(II, p. 573)

But while Flaubert is aware of the aesthetic potential of his almost autistic characteristics, of his ability to experience life as a dream, Maxime Du Camp reminds us that a particular value system is at work, which could be assessed quite differently. His evident disdain for the behaviour of his travelling companion highlights the uniqueness of Flaubert's enjoyment of 'mindless' passivity:

Gustave Flaubert n'avait rien de mon exaltation, il était calme et vivait en lui-même. Le mouvement, l'action lui étaient antipathiques. Il eût aimé à voyager, s'il eût pu, couché sur un divan et ne bougeant pas, voir les paysages, les ruines et les cités passer devant lui comme une toile de panorama qui se déroule mécaniquement [...] Les temples lui paraissaient toujours semblables, les mosquées toujours pareilles. (1964, p. 28)

Flaubert, who himself admits that he is fed up with all the temples,[13] quite explicitly corroborates Du Camp's account, but gives his own version of what is at stake:

On se dérange pour voir des ruines et des arbres; mais entre la ruine et l'arbre c'est tout autre chose que l'on rencontre; et de tout cela: paysages et canailleries, résulte en vous une pitié tranquille et indifférente, sérénité rêveuse qui promène son regard sans l'attacher sur rien parce que tout vous est égal et qu'on se sent aimer autant les bêtes que les hommes, et les galets de la mer autant que les maisons des villes. Pleine de couchers de soleil, de bruits de flots et de feuillages, et de senteurs de bois, et de troupeaux, avec des souvenirs de figures humaines dans toutes les postures et les grimaces du monde, l'âme recueillie sur elle-même sourit silencieusement en sa digestion, comme une bayadère engourdie d'opium. (*Corr.* (B) I, p. 746 (1851))

This illustrates admirably that Flaubert's supposed fascination with the local colour and whole 'côté moral' of his journey is far from that of the probing, curious tourist. The very way in which customs and people are described suggests that the aesthetic attitude is at work, and that in his claim 'peu d'étonnement de la nature [...] étonnement énorme des villes et des hommes' (*Corr.* (B) I, p. 538 (1849)), it is the quality of his reaction − astonishment − that should be extracted:

Mais ce qui excite, par exemple, ce sont les chameaux (les vrais, ceux qui ont quatre pattes) traversant les bazars; ce sont les mosquées avec leurs fontaines, les rues pleines de costumes de tous pays, les cafés qui regorgent de fumée de tabac et les places publiques retentissantes de baladins et de farceurs. Il y a sur tout cela, ou plutôt *c'est de tout cela que ressort une couleur d'enfer qui vous empoigne, un charme singulier qui vous tient bouche béante.*

(*Corr.* (B) I, p. 555 (1849), my emphasis)

17

Bains de Cléopâtre: petite anse dans la mer, avec les grottes à gauche.

> Toutes sortes de couleurs chatoyaient, le bord des roches dans l'eau était rouge, comme s'il y avait eu de la lie de vin répandue; un Arabe, pieds nus et retroussant sa robe, avancé dans l'eau jusqu'aux chevilles, nettoyait avec un couteau une peau de mouton. *Le soleil tapait sur tout cela, j'étais debout et muet.* (II, p. 558, my emphasis)

Attempted analytical observation invariably slips back into admiring, silent and immobile contemplation, which freezes its object into the perfect fusion of a real and an imagined tableau:

> les montagnes étaient lie de vin, le Nil bleu, le ciel outremer et les verdures d'un vert livide; tout était immobile; *ça avait l'air d'un paysage peint, d'un immense décor de théâtre fait exprès pour nous.* Quelques bons Turcs fumaient au pied des arbres avec leurs turbans et leurs longues pipes.
> (*Corr.* (B) I, p. 608 (1850), my emphasis)

In the right frame of mind the most commonplace action can be perceived as a beautiful gesture, and again and again Flaubert tries to pin down the subjective effect:

> L'homme à terre, allongeant le bras pour donner une poignée de main ou offrir quelque chose à l'homme monté sur son chameau, est un des plus beaux gestes orientaux; surtout au départ, il y a là quelque chose de solennel et de gravement triste. (II, p. 595)

> Une cange en tartane passe dessus: voilà le vrai Orient, effet mélancolique et endormant; vous pressentez déjà quelque chose d'immense et d'impitoyable, au milieu duquel vous êtes perdu. (p. 559)

There can be no doubt of Flaubert's enormous enjoyment of the solemn, melancholy effect of all the incidents resembling my initial point of reference, the meeting with the caravan, nor of the way such incidents are intimately tied up with his lasting image of 'le vrai Orient'.

If human beings, prostitutes and slaves are apprehended in exactly the same way as the desert and the much admired camels, it is certainly for the 'immuables' and 'inébranlables' qualities of arab *mores*, which Flaubert finds particularly conducive to his preferred mode of meditation:

> Je médite très peu, je rêvasse occasionnellement. − Mon genre d'observation est surtout moral. Je n'aurais jamais soupçonné ce côté au voyage. Le côté psychologique, humain, comique y est abondant. On rencontre des balles splendides, des existences gorge-pigeon très chatoyantes à l'œil, fort variées comme loques et broderies, riches de saletés, de déchirures et de galons. − Et au fond toujours cette vieille canaillerie immuable et inébranlable. C'est là la base. Ah! comme il vous en passe sous les yeux! (*Corr.* (B) I, pp. 707−8 (1850))

Oriental aesthetics

Consider Flaubert's description of a visit to one of the more elegant cafés in Cairo, one of those grotesque encounters which delight him beyond measure and of which he certainly tries to capture the flavour in many a later incident in his novels:

il y avait en même temps que nous, dans le café, un âne qui chiait et un monsieur qui pissait dans un coin. Personne ne trouve ça drôle, personne ne dit rien. Quelquefois un homme près de vous se lève et se met à dire sa prière, avec grandes prosternations et grandes exclamations, comme s'il était tout seul. On ne détourne même pas la tête. (*Corr.* (B) I, p. 584 (1850))

How could mere analysis ever get to the bottom of such a splendid moment? It is the very 'immutability' and 'unshatterability' which causes Flaubert to prize these incidents so highly, for theirs are the qualities that underlie his extraordinary belief in the aesthetic potential of 'la Bêtise',[14] of which Thompson of Sunderland's well-known contribution is but one example:

La bêtise est quelque chose d'inébranlable; rien ne l'attaque sans se briser contre elle. Elle est de la nature du granit, dure et résistante. À Alexandrie, un certain Thompson, de Sunderland, a sur la colonne de Pompée écrit son nom en lettres de six pieds de haut. Cela se lit à un quart de lieue de distance.
(*Corr.* (B) I, p. 689 (1850))

It is clear that many of Flaubert's famous declarations of aesthetic intent can be traced directly to his experience of the Orient. The 1852 meditation on Apuleius's *The Golden Ass* − Flaubert's artistic ideal is often best expressed where he tries to analyse his own literary admirations − is an excellent first example:

Il me donne à moi des vertiges et des éblouissements. La nature pour elle-même, le paysage, le côté purement pittoresque des choses sont traités là à la moderne et avec un souffle antique et chrétien tout ensemble qui passe au milieu. Ça sent l'encens et l'urine, la bestialité s'y marie au mysticisme, nous sommes bien loin encore de cela, nous autres, comme faisandage moral. Ce qui me fait croire que la littérature française est encore jeune! − Musset aime la gaudriole. Eh bien! pas moi. Elle sent l'esprit (que je l'exècre en art!). Les chefs-d'œuvre sont bêtes. − Ils ont la mine tranquille comme les productions mêmes de la nature, comme les grands animaux et les montagnes. J'aime l'ordure, oui, et quand elle est lyrique, comme dans Rabelais qui n'est point du tout un homme à gaudrioles. (*Corr.* (B) II, p. 119 (1852))

The effect on Flaubert ('des vertiges et des éblouissements') is very much that of the Orient, for example the *vertige* inspired by the Sphinx: 'Nous nous arrêtons devant le Sphinx, il nous regarde d'une façon terrifiante; Maxime est tout pâle, j'ai peur que la tête ne me

19

tourne et je tâche de dominer mon émotion' (II, p. 562). It is an effect he will aim to reproduce for his readers, so often referred to as spectators: 'que l'on sente dans tous les atomes, à tous les aspects, une impassibilité cachée et infinie. L'effet, pour le spectateur, doit être une espèce d'ébahissement. Comment tout cela s'est-il fait! doit-on dire! et qu'on se sente écrasé sans savoir pourquoi' (*Corr.* (B) II, p. 204 (1852)). This explains his enormous admiration for Rabelais and *Don Quixote*: 'Quels écrasants livres! Ils grandissent à mesure qu'on les contemple, comme les Pyramides, et on finit presque par avoir peur!' (p. 179). To describe his impression of an actual pyramid, Flaubert uses similes of towering natural scenery – 'ça a l'air d'une falaise, de quelque chose de la nature, d'une montagne qui serait faite comme cela, de je ne sais quoi de terrible qui va vous écraser' (II, p. 564) – while his well-known recommendation that art should aspire to 'agir à la façon de la nature, c'est-à-dire de *faire rêver*', picks up this imagery to convey a similar effect:

Aussi les très belles œuvres ont ce caractère. Elles sont sereines d'aspect et incompréhensibles. Quant au procédé, elles sont immobiles comme des falaises, houleuses comme l'Océan, pleine de frondaisons, de verdures et de murmures comme des bois, tristes comme le désert, bleues comme le ciel. Homère, Rabelais, Michel-Ange, Shakespeare, Goethe m'apparaissent *impitoyables*.   (*Corr.* (B) II, p. 417 (1853))

If I am right that such fundamental formulations of the ideal nature and effect of the novel are related to the experience of the Orient, it is perhaps appropriate to ask whether *Salammbô*, Flaubert's oriental (if historical) novel, may not be his closest approximation to this ideal. At an early stage in its writing Flaubert felt the need to revisit the Orient, and spent some part of his two-month stay on archaeological investigations at Tunis. Yet, back at Croisset and writing up his notes, Flaubert twice uses the image of a masked ball to sum up his memory of his stay, and it seems likely that this is precisely the impact of the Orient that he wished to revive:

Parti à midi; départ solennel: cinq cavaliers, puis sept; une vingtaine d'hommes à pied me suivent. C'est maintenant comme un bal masqué dans ma tête, je ne me souviens plus de rien.   (II, p. 718)

Voilà trois jours passés à peu près exclusivement à dormir. Mon voyage est considérablement reculé, oublié; tout est confus dans ma tête, je suis comme si je sortais d'un bal masqué de deux mois.   (p. 720)

From likening his visit to a masked ball he moves to the metaphor of a mirage (more desert vocabulary) to capture his central intention in the novel itself: 'J'ai voulu fixer un mirage en appliquant à l'antiquité les procédés du roman moderne' (*Corr.* (C) V, p. 56 (1862)), and discussing his refusal to allow illustrations, he refers to *Salammbô* as a 'dream': 'Ce n'était guère la peine d'employer tant d'art à laisser tout dans le vague, pour qu'un pignouf vienne démolir mon rêve par sa précision inepte' (p. 24). The polemic which arose over the accuracy of his historical details gave Flaubert the opportunity to spell out that he was only trying to create an 'image' of Carthage that would not contradict the French nineteenth-century received view of it by obvious inaccuracy or improbability:

Je crois avoir fait quelque chose qui ressemble à Carthage. Mais là n'est pas la question. Je me moque de l'archéologie! (*Corr.* (C) V, p. 67 (1862))

Dieu sait jusqu'à quel point je pousse le scrupule en fait de documents, livres, informations, voyages, etc. ... Eh bien, je regarde tout cela comme très secondaire et inférieur [...] Me croyez-vous assez godiche pour être convaincu que j'ai fait dans *Salammbô* une vraie reproduction de Carthage, et dans *Saint Antoine* une peinture exacte d'Alexandrinisme? Ah! non! mais je suis sûr d'avoir exprimé l'idéal qu'on en a aujourd'hui. (*Corr.* (C) VIII, p. 374 (1880))

Insisting here on the priority of the artistic illusion over the accuracy of the detail, Flaubert reasserts his belief that documentation is a secondary prop for the work of the imagination:

Voilà ce qui fait de l'observation artistique une chose bien différente de l'observation scientifique: elle doit surtout être instinctive et procéder par imagination, d'abord. Vous concevez un sujet, une couleur, et vous l'affermissez ensuite par des secours étrangers. (*Corr.* (B) II, p. 349 (1853))

But it seems likely that he relied heavily on these external aids, for despite his propensity to derealize his actual surroundings, he speaks of his difficulties in thinking up details of plot and of the enormous efforts of imagination required:[15] 'L'important avant tout est d'avoir des images nettes, de donner une illusion, or, pour y arriver, il faut une abondance de plans secondaires dans lesquels je m'embourbe' (*Corr. Suppl.* I, p. 233 (1857)). Ideally he has recourse to written props, and the Goncourt brothers, always acute in their preceptions of Flaubert, comment on the laboriously applied ingenuity of this method of work which seeks so paradoxically to build an illusion with plans and notes.[16] *La Tentation de Saint Antoine* is described as 'de l'imagination faite avec des notes' (1956, II, p. 974), and *Salammbô* as: 'une invention pas vraisemblable, une déduction de toutes les couleurs locales des civilisations antiques et orientales, très ingénieuse et qui arrive par son profusion de tons et de parfums à être quelque chose d'entêtant' (I, p. 889). But the Goncourts are disappointed ultimately because Flaubert's monotonous methods produce 'une lassitude où l'attention roule et se perd' (p. 913). Yet their resulting 'étourdissement' (p. 912) was certainly intended by Flaubert, who openly dubs *Salammbô* a 'lourd roman' (*Corr. Suppl.* I, p. 266 (undated)), and 'embêtante à crever' (*Corr.* (C) IV, p. 440 (1861)) – the deliberate heaviness is the essential quality for lulling the reader into the dazed state in which he will be most amenable to the claims of reverie. Indeed Flaubert states unequivocally that he wishes to subject the reader to an exclusively aesthetic experience:

> Le livre que j'écris maintenant sera tellement loin des mœurs modernes qu'aucune ressemblance entre mes héros et les lecteurs n'étant possible, il intéressera fort peu. On n'y verra aucune observation, rien de ce qu'on aime généralement. Ce sera de l'Art, de l'Art pur et pas autre chose.
>
> (*Corr.* (B) II, p. 794 (1858))[17]

This general remoteness and inaccessibility is increased by Flaubert's frequent recourse to a shifting narrative viewpoint which I would suggest is used, in this novel at least, to undermine empathy. For whereas in any 'epic' war novel – or film – an inner view of both warring parties is an almost clichéd way of involving the viewer in both sides, in *Salammbô*, though this inevitably happens to a certain extent, the constant switches from the following of events with one side to the sudden sharing of an external viewpoint (and even more obviously, a long shot) upon them, tends to increase rather than to break down strangeness. Thus the crucified lions cause the Barbarians a 'long étonnement' (I, p. 702), and the sacrifice of the Carthaginian children (which the reader had followed from a Carthaginian standpoint), seen suddenly through the mercenaries' eyes, leaves them 'béants d'horreur' (p. 781). On the other hand the mortal combat between the remaining Barbarians in the Défilé de la Hache, described at first in almost moving terms, is then subjected to a similar estrangement: 'leur délire était si furieux que les Carthaginois, de loin, avaient peur' (p. 788). Thus all languages, races, customs, and even the main characters are rendered opaque (with distant shots of Salammbô, Mâtho, Spendius and Hamilcar),[18] and this device contributes to the aesthetic impact of the novel, conceived by Flaubert as a dense and impenetrable object.

The first appearance of Salammbô at the feast establishes a context of *mutual* incomprehension and hence 'ébahissement':

> Les soldats, sans comprendre ce qu'elle disait, se tassaient autour d'elle. Ils s'ébahissaient de sa parure; mais elle promena sur eux tous un long regard

épouvanté, puis s'enfonçant la tête dans les épaules en écartant les bras, elle répéta plusieurs fois:
— Qu'avez-vous fait! qu'avez-vous fait!   (p. 697)

The use of the exclamation mark rather than a question mark after 'Qu'avez-vous fait', and the repetition of the phrase, imply stunned amazement rather than a desire for knowledge. Although Salammbô is described as wishing to penetrate the depths of the dogma of Tanit, dull incomprehension dominates all her attempts. She learns Tanit's adventures and various names, and repeats them over and over 'sans qu'ils eussent pour elle de signification distincte', while the following exchange with Schahabarim is typical of her 'lessons':

— Elle inspire et gouverne les amours des hommes.
— Les amours des hommes! répéta Salammbô en rêvant.   (p. 709)

The effect of Salammbô on Mâtho is described as 'une surprise infinie, un étourdissement' (p. 766), and their encounters are imbued with 'béance' and reverie:

— C'est le voile de la Déesse!
— Le voile de la Déesse! s'écria Salammbô [...] ils restèrent béants à se regarder.
Sans comprendre ce qu'il sollicitait, une horreur la saisit.   (p. 720)

As Taanach prepares Salammbô for her mission to Mâtho this atmosphere of reverie intensifies:

— Tu ne seras pas plus belle le jour de tes noces!
— Mes noces! répéta Salammbô; elle rêvait, le coude appuyé sur la chaise d'ivoire.   (p. 756)

But it is above all the scene in the tent which is marked by a whole series of stupefied, uncomprehending, incantatory repetitions:

Il la regardait de bas en haut, en la tenant ainsi entre ses jambes, et il répétait:
— Comme tu es belle! comme tu es belle!   (p. 758)

— A moins, peut-être, que tu ne sois Tanit?
— Moi, Tanit? se disait Salammbô [...]
Une lassitude l'accablait; elle écoutait avec stupeur le cri intermittent des sentinelles qui se répondaient [...]
— Je m'en retourne à Carthage [...]
— T'en retourner à Carthage! Il balbutiait, et répétait, en griçant des dents:
— T'en retourner à Carthage!   (p. 759)

The material quality of language, so essential to this gaping incomprehension, is constantly underlined by reference to the many different foreign languages of the mercenaries, and by the recourse to exotic foreign words and names ('Siv! Sivan! Tammouz, Eloul, Tischri, Schebar!' (p. 697), 'A moi, Taanach, Kroûm, Ewa, Micipsa, Schoûl' (p. 720)), which may be seen, along with the textual repetitions, as an incitement to reverie in the reader. The inevitable 'torpeur' ('dans une invincible torpeur, comme ceux qui ont pris autrefois quelque breuvage dont ils doivent mourir'), and 'accablement' ('un accablement qui était plein de délices') (p. 703), were doubtless conceived by Flaubert as pleasurable states (the Goncourts' reaction notwithstanding). Salammbô, who was already suitably unhinged from reality, derealizes for herself her love-tryst with Mâtho: 'tout cela, du reste, flottait dans sa tête, mélancolique et brumeux, comme le souvenir d'un rêve accablant' (p. 773). Even the most reality-bound of readers will be unable to avoid processing this *story* of the *memory* of a *dream* in anything but the aesthetic attitude, or submitting docilely to the fascination of the 'image' of Mâtho:

> toutes les choses extérieures s'effaçant, elle n'avait aperçu que Mâtho. Un silence s'était fait dans son âme, un de ces abîmes où le monde entier disparaît sous la pression d'une pensée unique, d'un souvenir, d'un regard. Cet homme, qui marchait vers elle, l'attirait. (p. 796)

For 'fascination' is probably the best word to sum up the passive gaping that Flaubert thematizes through the uncomprehending attitude of his characters to each other, to the world, and to language, and which might be seen as an ideal model for the reader's relationship to the novel.[19]

2

THE MERITS OF INARTICULACY

Although his 'weak vessels' have often attracted critical disapproval, Flaubert himself suggests an important connection between moral and aesthetic values in so-called 'simple' characters:

> Les mots sublimes (que l'on rapporte dans les histoires) ont été dits souvent par des simples. Ce qui n'est nullement un argument contre l'Art, au contraire, car ils avaient ce qui fait l'Art même, à savoir la pensée concrétée, un sentiment quelconque, *violent*, et arrivé à son dernier état d'idéal. 'Si vous aviez la foi, vous remuerez des montagnes' est aussi le principe du Beau.
>
> (*Corr.* (B) II, p. 785 (1957))

Flaubert writes into his works an almost explicit argument on behalf of such characters, whose simplicity invariably takes the form of an extreme linguistic disadvantage. If language itself is sometimes blamed for difficulties of self-expression,[1] inarticulate characters are more usually seen to have a personal problem. It is not that the right words do not exist, but that they do not have access to them. They are not good at translating their experience of the world into speech, and are especially unable to use language to communicate with other people. Nor is this because their thoughts are too profound for expression – the same characters clearly lack intellectual capacity as well. Yet Flaubert uses them to incarnate positive values such as single-mindedness, silence, immobility and imaginative sympathy. These values seem, in Flaubert, to possess a traditional moral sense, but all also have aesthetic connotations. At the same time, Flaubert undermines, at the level of theme and plot, the normally accepted function of spoken language as an instrument of self-expression and communication. He does this through a debunking of various forms of verbal facility, accompanied by a sustained caricature of any intellectual outlook on the world as boring pedantry.

Sartre's influential analysis of the ubiquitous but slippery concept of 'la Bêtise' (*L'Idiot* I, pp. 612–48) suggests that it originates as a quality of language, but is best characterized as a refusal to synthesize

25

— stupidity is basically an attitude which makes things stupid. It is powerful because no position can be adopted to combat it, that is, its identification has nothing to do with formulating a more sensible alternative view (for example, opposing sound opinions to the silly ones of the bourgeoisie). Intelligence is neither a foil for stupidity nor an analytical weapon against it, but is invariably put forward by Flaubert as a sub-species of stupidity itself. Herein lies all the subtle difference between Balzac's treatment of a bourgeois fool like Célestin Crevel in *La Cousine Bette* and Flaubert's of M. Homais. For as Sartre suggests in an outstanding analysis of Homais, Flaubert's master-stroke is to make Homais the incarnation of intelligence (p. 642).

A fierce criticism of easy eloquence, verbosity, and pedantry is pursued right through Flaubert's works. He claims to have no liking for 'les doctrinaires d'aucune espèce' (*Corr. Suppl.* IV, p. 84 (1878)), and describes eloquence as 'une chose qui me laisse absolument froid' (*Corr. Suppl.* IV, p. 63 (1878)). This is a personal position maintained throughout his life and declared as early as 1837:

Il y a des jours où je donnerais toute la science des bavards passés, présents, futurs, toute la sotte érudition des éplucheurs, équarisseurs, philosophes, romanciers, chimistes, épiciers, académiciens, pour deux vers de Lamartine ou de Victor Hugo. Me voilà devenu bien anti-prose, anti-raison, anti-vérité car qu'est-ce que le beau sinon l'impossible, la poésie si ce n'est la barbarie — le cœur de l'homme. (*Corr.* (B) I, pp. 24–5)

He builds into his fiction a long line of complacent smooth talkers: Ernest, Paul and the later Henry prefigure the better-known examples of Lheureux and Rodolphe. Flaubert's method is often to set up a contrast between a pair of characters, whereby some version of pompous verbosity acts as a foil for apparent ignorance, ineloquence or simplicity. Straightforward examples abound in a rather obvious way in the early works.

Giacomo, the illiterate, manic book collector of *Bibliomanie* is above all a silent man, apparently by choice: 'Cet homme n'avait jamais parlé à personne, si ce n'est aux bouquinistes et aux brocanteurs; il était taciturne et rêveur' (I, p. 78). This causes him to be despised and misunderstood, but, standing in court accused of arson, theft and murder: 'il était calme et paisible, et ne répondit pas même par un regard à la multitude qui l'insultait'. This dignified silence is set in relief by the nature of the prosecutor's speech which precedes it: 'le Procureur se leva et lut son rapport; il était long et diffus, à peine si on pouvait en distinguer l'action principale des parenthèses et des réflexions', and that of his own 'clever' lawyer — 'il parla

longtemps et bien; enfin, quand il crut avoir ébranlé son auditoire
...' – who makes the tactical error of producing the second Bible
(I, p. 82).

In *Quidquid volueris* a clear contrast is set up between Djalioh and
Paul. Djalioh cannot read or write, and while it is not made clear
whether he is actually dumb, he appears to be so for all practical purposes. He cannot make himself understood, and although the narrator
suggests that his strange and incoherent violin music at the wedding
is some form of self-expression, this music in no way explains him
to his audience: 'Tout le monde se mit à rire, tant la musique était
fausse, bizarre, incohérente' (I, p. 108). Yet the richness which lies
behind his inarticulacy is made explicit for the reader:

Si c'était un mot ou un soupir, peu importe, mais il y avait là-dedans toute
une âme! [...] Oh! son cœur était vaste et immense, mais vaste comme la mer,
immense et vide comme sa solitude [...] Il avait en lui un chaos des sentiments
les plus étranges; la poésie avait remplacé la logique, et les passions avaient
pris la place de la science.   (pp. 104–5)

He is all poetry, passion and capacity for love, while Paul is a cold,
rational person, who has even created Djalioh by way of a scientific
experiment: 'l'homme sensé, celui qu'on respecte et qu'on honore;
car il monte sa garde nationale, s'habille comme tout le monde, parle
morale et philanthropie' (p. 103). Paul translates his shallow feelings
into easy words, while Djalioh's experience remains non-verbal and
unformulated, and Flaubert heavily underlines the moral lesson which
he means his reader to draw from the contrasts:

Voilà le monstre de la nature qui était en contact avec M. Paul, cet autre
monstre, ou plutôt cette merveille de la civilisation, et qui en portait tous les
symboles, grandeurs de l'esprit, sécheresse du cœur. Autant l'un avait d'amour
pour les épanchements de l'âme, les douces causeries du cœur, autant Djalioh
aimait les rêveries de la nuit et les songes de la pensée [...] où l'intelligence
finissait, le cœur prenait son empire; il était vaste et infini, car il comprenait le
monde dans son amour.   (p. 105)

Mazza and Ernest, of *Passion et vertu*, an obvious first sketch of
Emma and Rodolphe, represent the same dichotomy, for Mazza lives
in a world of emotion, while Ernest is all judgement and reason:
'C'était un de ces gens chez qui le jugement et la raison occupent une
si grande place qu'ils ont mangé le cœur comme un voisin incommode'
(I, p. 120). Like Rodolphe, Ernest is a skilful talker who knows how
to exploit language for purposes of seduction, how to flatter Mazza
and to out-argue her scruples:

27

— Il faut que je l'aime. [her husband]

— Cela est plus facile à dire qu'à faire, c'est-à-dire que si la loi vous dit: 'Vous l'aimerez', votre cœur s'y pliera comme un régiment qu'on fait manœuvrer ou une barre d'acier qu'on ploie des deux mains, et si moi je vous aime... [...] il faudra que je ne vous aime plus parce qu'il le faudra, et rien de plus; mais cela est-il sensé et juste?

— Ah! vous raisonnez à merveille, mon cher ami.   (pp. 114–15)

Once he feels the need he can even persuade himself out of any feelings of love he may have (again resembling Rodolphe regretfully renouncing Emma): 'La lettre était longue, bien écrite, toute remplie de riches métaphores et de grands mots ... Pauvre Mazza! tant d'amour, de cœur et de tendresse pour une indifférence si froide, un calme si raisonné!' (p. 119). The young Flaubert cannot resist spelling out the moral lesson behind the contrast of eloquence and ineloquence: 'Quel trésor que l'amour d'une telle femme!' (p. 123).

In the 1845 *L'Éducation sentimentale* Alvarès's silent love for Mlle Aglaé rings what is beginning to sound like a typical note: 'il aurait épuisé l'éternité à tourner, comme un cheval au manège, autour de cette idée fixe et immobile, il n'en parlait plus, mais dans le silence de son cœur il se consumait solitairement' (I, p. 319). And Flaubert comes near to doing something important with Shahutsnischbach, who is not just awkward but arguably Flaubert's first really stupid character. He makes his *début* arriving late at Mme Renaud's dinner party, in his everyday clothes and covered in chalk: 'étonné, confus, ébahi, ne sachant s'il devait s'en aller ou rester, s'enfuir ou s'asseoir, les bras ballants, le nez au vent, ahuri, stupide' (p. 286). Later we learn why Shahutsnischbach is the only young man of the household not to be in love: 'il travaillait toujours aux mathématiques, les mathématiques dévorait sa vie, il n'y comprenait rien. Jamais M. Renaud n'avait eu de jeune homme plus studieux... ni plus stupide; Mendès lui-même le regardait comme un butor' (p. 293). When M. Renaud makes a silly joke: 'Alvarès et Mendès rirent, Shahutsnischbach ne comprit pas' (p. 295), and at Mme Renaud's ball the stupid but good-natured German: 'resté dans l'anti-chambre, aidait les domestiques à passer les plateaux de la salle à manger dans le salon' (p. 301). For in the strange interlude where Henry sadistically 'beats up' M. Renaud in the street, Shahutsnischbach, who happens to be passing ('pour une commission que Mme Renaud lui envoyait faire'), shows a contrasting kindness:

Et le bon Allemand, en effet, le réconfortait de son mieux, il alla lui-même dans la cour, y mouilla son mouchoir sous la pompe, revint auprès de

The merits of inarticulacy

M. Renaud et lui essuya le sang qui était resté le long de sa figure; il s'offrit pour courir lui chercher un médecin, pour acheter quelque drogue s'il en avait besoin, pour aller avertir chez lui, pour tout ce qu'il voudrait, n'importe quoi. En songeant que, jusqu'à cette heure, à peine s'il l'avait regardé et qu'il le méprisait même pour son manque d'esprit, le père Renaud se sentait le cœur navré et était pris de l'envie de le serrer dans ses bras, de l'embrasser comme son fils.   (p. 349)

Built into the final development of Henry and Jules is a very marked contrast between verbal facility and its lack. Henry ends up by becoming a man of the world, only really believing in feelings which can be expressed. His superficial intelligence is characterized by its easy processing of language:

Il croit bien connaître le théâtre, parce qu'il saisit à première vue toutes les ficelles d'un mélodrame et les intentions d'une exposition [...] il passe pour avoir le tact fin, car il découvrira l'épithète heureuse, le trait saillant ou le mot hasardeux qui fait tache [...]

Il a un avantage sur ceux qui voient plus loin et qui sentent d'une façon plus intense, c'est qu'il peut justifier ses sensations et donner la preuve de ses assertions; il expose nettement ce qu'il éprouve, il écrit clairement ce qu'il pense, et dans le développement d'une théorie comme dans la pratique d'un sentiment, il écrase les natures plus engagées dans l'infini, chez lesquelles l'idée chante et la passion rêve.   (p. 365)

Such articulacy is typically combined with a complete inability to understand people different from himself, and of this, we know, Flaubert disapproves:

Il n'estimait pas ceux qui se grisent avec de l'eau-de-vie, parce qu'il préférait le vin: il trouvait le goût de la pipe trop fort, parce qu'il fumait des cigarettes [...] il ne comprenait pas les gens qui meurent d'amour, lui qui avait tant aimé et qui n'en était pas mort.   (p. 364)

But his opposite, Jules, is shown to have moved right away from the verbal domain, especially as an artist: 'la discussion lui était devenue impossible, il n'y avait à son usage de mode de transmission psychologique que l'expansion, la communication directe, l'inspiration simultanée' (p. 360).

Playing the various characters of *Madame Bovary* off against each other is an altogether more complicated business, largely because of the ambivalent treatment of Emma and Charles. A clear undermining of pompous verbosity is nevertheless apparent, which sets in relief some famous worldless characters. At the very centre of the novel (middle chapter of middle part), Flaubert inserts, in the set-piece 'symphony' of the agricultural show, the description of the old peasant woman receiving her medal. Catherine Leroux is often commented upon, normally to emphasize the contrast between the complacent bourgeoisie and 'ce demi-siècle de servitude' (I, p. 625). But I should prefer to underline her silence and immobility. By frequenting farm animals all her life she has assumed their dumb placidity. Whereas the gaping crowd is shown drinking in the ridiculous speeches against a background of mooing cows, Catherine Leroux is so frightened by the noise, bustle and confusion, that her reaction is simply to stand quite still, not knowing what else to do. In a scene carefully constructed so as to oppose the absurd parallel exploitation of the official speeches (to seduce the crowd), and of Rodolphe (to seduce Emma) – both are shown to be equally effective – the implicit moral worth of the old woman who does not even understand language is foregrounded, the more so given the reaction of the audience: '— Ah! qu'elle est bête!'. Abuse of language for various reasons is so widespread throughout the novel (Lheureux's selling technique, Homais's journalistic powers, the campaign to persuade Charles to operate on the club-foot), that characters who hardly speak should be prized by the reader quite simply for not misusing language.

M. Homais's view of the relative values of silence and speech is made clear on his first appearance in the novel, through his disdain for Binet's uncommunicativeness:

pendant tout le temps que l'on fut à mettre son couvert, Binet resta silencieux à sa place, auprès du poêle; puis il ferma la porte et retira sa casquette, comme d'usage.
Ce ne sont pas les civilités qui lui useront la langue! dit le pharmacien, dès qu'il fut seul avec l'hôtesse.
— Jamais il ne cause davantage, répondit-elle; il est venu ici, la semaine dernière, deux voyageurs en draps, des garçons pleins d'esprit qui contaient, le soir, un tas de farces que j'en pleurais de rire: eh bien! il restait là, comme une alose, sans dire un mot.
— Oui, fit le pharmacien, pas d'imagination, pas de saillies, rien de ce qui constitue l'homme de la société! (p. 600)

The particular combination of talkativeness and useless knowledge that distinguishes Homais throughout the novel is characterized by his preferred version of social intercourse with the Bovarys:

Ensuite, on causait de ce qu'il y avait *dans le journal*. Homais, à cette heure-là, le savait presque par cœur; et il le rapportait intégralement, avec les réflexions du journaliste et toutes les histoires des catastrophes individuelles arrivées en France ou à l'étranger. Mais le sujet se tarissant, il ne tardait pas à lancer quelques observations sur les mets qu'il voyait. Parfois même, se levant à demi, il indiquait délicatement à Madame le morceau le plus tendre, ou, se tournant vers la bonne, lui adressait des conseils, pour la manipulation des ragoûts et l'hygiène des assaisonnements; il parlait arome, osmazôme, suc et gélatine d'une façon à éblouir.

(p. 607)

Flaubert takes particular pleasure in deflating Homais when he is given the task of breaking the news that Emma's father-in-law has died: 'Il avait médité sa phrase, il l'avait arrondie, polie, rhythmée, c'était un chef-d'œuvre de prudence et de transition, de tournures fines et de délicatesse; mais la colère avait emporté la rhétorique' (p. 659). Perhaps the abrupt outburst which is substituted in the event is a salutary one, for when Homais writes to Emma's father to tell him she is dead: 'par égard pour sa sensibilité, M. Homais l'avait rédigée de telle façon qu'il était impossible de savoir à quoi s'en tenir' (p. 687). The preferability of Père Rouault's own uneducated style of letter-writing is surely apparent: 'Les fautes d'orthographe s'y enlaçaient les unes aux autres, et Emma poursuivait la pensée douce qui caquetait tout au travers comme une poule à demi cachée dans une haie d'épine' (p. 632).

Charles's generally distracted and wordless grief makes the ending of the novel moving in a way that Flaubert quite explicitly intended,[2] and it is only when 'il la regardait avec des yeux d'une tendresse comme elle n'en avait jamais vu' that Emma at last consecrates his value with her 'tu es bon, toi!' (p. 681). Indeed one interpretation of the finding of the autopsy on Charles would surely be that he is allowed the fictional privilege of dying of a broken heart. Less dramatic than Salammbô's death, it is equally strongly motivated, and the cruelly ambiguous 'Il l'ouvrit et ne trouva rien' (p. 692), which both sets the seal on his moral worth and on his 'stupidity', captures the possible connection between the two.

Critics have more readily noticed that Charles speaks in clichés than that such a central character can barely speak at all. In the first part of the novel, despite his large part in the plot, he is especially wordless — direct conversations that exist in the early drafts have been removed by Flaubert to give greater emphasis to Charles's occasional stutterings.[3] It is not that he is a secretive, deliberately silent person; by nature he is relatively expansive and tells Emma everything. He simply has no command of language. The famous 'Charbovari' scene presents a lasting image of Charles: introduced to the reader as 'un nom inintelligible' (p. 575), he cannot even pronounce his own name. He is aware of his own problem to the extent that he dare not ask for Emma's hand in marriage: 'la peur de ne point trouver les mots convenables lui collait les lèvres' (p. 582). Indeed he is right and when the moment comes can manage only to stammer out 'Père Rouault... Père Rouault'. If he is a social failure at his wedding it is because he is unable to keep up with the jokes, puns and obligatory allusions, for their medium is linguistic. In fact in so far as Charles is transformed by the wedding night, it is his powers of speech that are temporarily improved: 'Mais Charles ne dissimulait rien. Il l'appelaient ma femme, la tutoyait, s'informait d'elle à chacun' (p. 584).

Though Emma's language is clichéd and while her tragedy is partly tied up with the misunderstanding or abuse of words, she is not properly speaking inarticulate, and is quite at home in a verbal atmosphere. In many ways she serves as a contrast for Charles here. While Charles is totally nonplussed by his medical studies and can only pass his examinations by learning the answers by heart, Emma can understand all the difficult parts of the catechism at school, and can send out well-phrased letters to Charles's clients. She notices and easily fits into the social conventions at La Vaubyessard, whereas Charles spends five hours at the card tables 'à regarder jouer au whist, sans y rien comprendre' (p. 592). The first reported conversation between them shows how easily Emma can out-argue Charles:

> — Les sous-pieds vont me gêner pour danser, dit-il.
> — Danser? reprit Emma.
> — Oui!
> — Mais tu as perdu la tête! on se moquerait de toi, reste à ta place.
> D'ailleurs, c'est plus convenable pour un médecin, ajouta-t-elle.
> Charles se tut.   (p. 591)

It is because Emma needs to converse with someone that she becomes dissatisfied with Charles, and although at first she wishes that he would understand her need, she more or less writes him off for good when 'il ne put, un jour, lui expliquer un terme d'équitation qu'elle avait rencontré dans un roman' (p. 588).

Flaubert points out that Emma is at least partly seduced by Rodolphe's verbal 'galanterie': 'C'était la première fois qu'Emma s'entendait dire ces choses; et son orgueil, comme quelqu'un qui se délasse dans une étuve, s'étirait mollement et tout entier à la chaleur de ce langage' (p. 627). It is because Charles is so incapable of using the clichéd language of love with which she is familiar that she can never understand that he loves her (Flaubert's rough notes state plainly that Charles adores Emma far more than Léon and Rodolphe ever do, and that though clumsy and without imagination, he is 'sensible' (Pommier and Leleu, 1949, pp. 3 and 21)). Emma's most serious

personal failing is her inability to understand any experi
than her own: 'guère tendre, cependant, ni facilement acc
l'émotion d'autrui' (p. 597), and:

incapable, du reste, de comprendre ce qu'elle n'éprouvait pas, comme d
croire à tout ce qui ne se manifestait point par des formes convenues, elle
se persuada sans peine que la passion de Charles n'avait plus rien d'exhorbi-
tant. Ses expansions étaient devenues régulières; il l'embrassait à de certaines
heures.
(p. 589)

At the climax of her disgust with him she denigrates him as 'cet homme
qui ne comprenait rien, qui ne sentait rien!' (p. 637), and her mistake
is obviously supposed to lie in thinking that the two activities of
intellectual understanding and feeling have any necessary connection.
Critical discussions of Charles as the clumsy and stupid husband who
cannot cater for Emma's needs therefore miss at least half of the
point. This was spelled out by Flaubert in a grandiloquent description
of Charles to be found in earlier versions of the novel. In this passage
– deleted perhaps for the very reason that it overemphasizes one *half*
of the final, ambivalent Charles – Rodolphe, at their final meeting,
scorns Charles for not hating him:

Car il ne comprenait rien à cet amour vorace se précipitant au hasard sur les
choses pour s'assouvir, à la passion vide d'orgueil, sans respect humain, ni
conscience, qui plonge tout entière dans l'être aimé, accapare ses sentiments,
en palpite, et touche presque aux proportions d'une idée pure, à force de
largeur et d'impersonnalité.   (Pommier and Leleu, 1949, p. 641)

This is precisely the treasured moral ideal of universal sympathy which
Emma lacks:[4] 'Il fallait qu'elle pût retirer des choses une sorte de
profit personnel; et elle rejetait comme inutile tout ce qui ne contri-
buait pas à la consommation immédiate de son cœur, – étant de
tempérament plus sentimentale qu'artiste' (I, p. 586). In fact my own
reading of the much glossed 'c'est la faute de la fatalité' (p. 692) would
be that if it is the ultimate cliché it is also the ultimate act of generosity.
For as seen in his wishes for her burial and in his much changed
behaviour after her death, Charles more or less succeeds in understanding Emma, 'raising' his ideals to the level of literary romances,
passionate affairs etc. These words could be seen to represent the final
insight into her world and are a generous self-sacrifice, for Charles
himself is not so trite.

But one character is ahead of Charles in understanding Emma's
value system, for her desire for a tilbury and groom is attributed to
Justin: 'C'était Justin qui lui en avait inspiré le caprice, en la suppliant

comme valet de chambre' (p. 665). Indeed if

Léon and Rodolphe, lies awake all night after

Justin's grief which is given the privileged

ng at the graveside. Justin is Charles's silent

s his values, and, as Flaubert makes quite

o offers adoring but unvoiced devotion of

ware: 'Elle ne se doutait point que l'amour,

là, près d'elle, sous cette chemise de grosse

scent ouvert aux émanations de sa beauté'

(p. 647). He is almost a caricature of Charles in that he is even more incompetent linguistically.[5] When Homais calls him a 'petit sot' for fainting 'Justin ne répondait pas' (p. 618), when in disgrace over the key to the arsenic his only response to Homais's noisy scene and 'Parle, réponds, articule quelque chose?' (p. 658) is a few stutterings, and his copy of *L'Amour conjugal* (like the geography book that provides Félicité's literary education in *Un Cœur simple*), needs pictures by way of explanation. He comes and goes so quietly that it is indeed easy to overlook him: 'Il montait avec eux dans la chambre, et il restait debout près de la porte, immobile, sans parler' (p. 647). Just as on the Sunday expedition to the flax mill his role is to carry the umbrellas and to wipe the children's shoes clean, his devotion is never articulated, but (again like Félicité's), shows itself in acts of service: 'et Justin, qui se trouvait là, circulait à pas muets, plus ingénieux à la servir qu'une excellente cámériste. Il plaçait les allumettes, le bougeoir, un livre, disposait sa camisole, ouvrait les draps' (p. 665). As this reference to the sheets suggests, it is the erotic and sensuous qualities of Emma which fascinate him, for example her hair, and it could be suggested that he shares with Charles the role of creating and preserving Emma's 'mystery', even when her rather silly interior has been made available to the reader. Justin's greatest satisfaction is always to watch Emma, and his imaginative sympathy has the power to transform reality: 'Et aussitôt il atteignit sur le chambranle les chaussures d'Emma tout empâtées de crotte — la crotte des rendez-vous — qui se détachait en poudre sous se doigts, et qu'il regardait monter doucement dans un rayon de soleil' (p. 638). That Flaubert regards this power as an artist's privilege is suggested when he writes to Maupassant: 'La poésie, comme le soleil, met l'or sur le fumier' (*Corr.* (C) VIII, p. 397 (1880)).

The values associated with inarticulate characters — silence, stillness and single-mindedness — are clearly built into the presentation of character in the 1869 *L'Éducation sentimentale*. The simple but loyal Dussardier, though a minor character, appears at enough crucial points in the novel to act as a symbol for its guiding moral thread. He is introduced stammering 'Où est mon carton? Je veux mon carton [...] Mon carton!' (II, p. 19), he is incapable of understanding the stories by means of which Frédéric and Hussonnet try to help him out of trouble at the police station, and his erudition is limited to two books. But his dream is to love one woman for life, his hatred for authority is unswerving, and, more faithful than his friends to his earlier cry of 'Vive la République!' (p. 114), he is struck down on 2nd December as he towers above the police in a quite immobile pose: 'un homme, – Dussardier, – remarquable de loin à sa haute taille, restait sans plus bouger qu'une cariatide' (p. 160). He is rewarded in the next line with a martyr's death: 'Il tomba sur le dos, les bras en croix.' [6]

Frédéric's persistent attachment to Mme Arnoux may well act on the reader as it does on Deslauriers: 'La persistance de cet amour l'irritait comme un problème. Son austérité un peu théâtrale l'ennuyait maintenant' (p. 97). Yet Frédéric's story embodies a deliberate tension between concentrated and diffuse experience, as he dabbles in painting, literature, business and politics, frittering his energies among four women between whom he seems unable to choose. Arnoux, Rosanette and many of Frédéric's Parisian acquaintances clearly provide the temptation of diffusion, and the semi-fidelity despite everything to Mme Arnoux is surely, in this context, a positive force. Part of Flaubert's problem is to build moral value into Mme Arnoux, despite her husband and, up to a point, despite Frédéric himself. This he does through the particular nature of Frédéric's perception of her, and through her place in the structure of the novel. By constructing the novel around her (through a complicated network of reminders), he obliges the reader to join in Frédéric's original desire to 'vivre dans son atmosphère' (p. 26), an atmosphere which is not only poetic and emotional, but essentially moral: 'la contemplation de cette femme l'énervait, comme l'usage d'un parfum trop fort. Cela descendit dans les profondeurs de son tempérament, et devenait presque une manière générale de sentir, un mode nouveau d'exister' (p. 33).

If Frédéric's 'Je n'ai jamais aimé qu'elle!' is less than totally convincing (p. 157), Mme Arnoux is nevertheless presented to the reader as a coherent force in the novel. The varieties of dispersion which act as a foil for her simplicity are invariably related to noise and unnecessary speech. Without being inarticulate Mme Arnoux is basically quiet, gentle and unaffected. Criticized by Frédéric for using bourgeois maxims, she protests that she has no pretensions to anything else. She has no special love of literature, she uses straightforward language, she is superstitious — 'croyait aux songes' (p. 38) — and enjoys commonplace pleasures like walking bareheaded in the rain. The very first vision of her is presented against a background of the noise, bustle and confusion of the departure of the boat. The talkative Arnoux fits naturally into this scene, involving everyone around him in his fragmentary conversation, giving advice, expounding theories, relating anecdotes. Mme Arnoux's 'apparition' is immediately preceded by a squalid description of the mess on the deck, of the noise and constant movement of the passengers and the captain:

Le pont était sali par des écales de noix, des bouts de cigares, des pelures de poires, des détritus de charcuterie apportée dans du papier [...] on entendait par intervalles le bruit du charbon de terre dans le fourneau, un éclat de voix, un rire; et le capitaine, sur la passerelle, marchait d'un tambour à l'autre, sans s'arrêter. (p. 9)

While everyone else mixes, laughing, joking and drinking together, dressed in old, worn and dirty travelling clothes, Mme Arnoux sits alone and silent, her light-coloured dress standing out against the blue sky. She is sewing, that is doing something useful, but above all she is still. Frédéric observes her for some minutes in the same pose, and on his last view of her as the boat arrives: 'Elle était près du gouvernail, debout. Il lui envoya un regard où il avait tâché de mettre toute son âme; comme s'il n'eût rien fait, elle demeura immobile' (p. 11). The immobile pose of this first scene is established almost as a leitmotif which appears throughout the novel, and on one occasion the continuity is even pointed out: 'Elle se tenait dans la même attitude que le premier jour, et cousait une chemise d'enfant' (p. 56). That these values are not necessarily obvious ones is shown up in the scene where Deslauriers dismisses his mistress: 'Elle se planta devant la fenêtre, et y resta immobile, le front contre le carreau. Son attitude et son mutisme agaça Deslauriers' (p. 73).

One especially memorable tableau of Mme Arnoux is during her fête at Saint-Cloud, where she is placed on a rock with a flaming sunset behind her, while the other guests wander around somewhat aimlessly, and Hussonnet on the river bank skims stones on the water. In his correspondence Flaubert twice uses this as an image to imply moral dispersion: 'Ah! mes richesses morales! J'ai jeté aux passants les grosses pièces par la fenêtre, et avec les louis j'ai fait des ricochets sur l'eau' (*Corr.* (B) I, p. 290 (1846)). Louise Colet's idea of a communally directed review is dismissed in the same terms: 'On bavarde beaucoup, on dépense tout son talent à faire des ricochets sur la rivière avec de la menue monnaie, tandis qu'avec plus d'économie on aurait

pu par la suite acheter de belles fermes et de bons châteaux' (C
(B) II, p. 291 (1853)). Appropriately it is Hussonnet who is chosei
to skim stones, for as the newspaper owner he emerges as a rival to
Mme Arnoux for Frédéric's time, attention and money. At Rosanette's
ball he is made by Flaubert to stand in Frédéric's line of vision and
thus to interrupt his thoughts – as the sight of the chandelier from
the *Art industriel* stirs old memories of Mme Arnoux, Frédéric is
suddenly distracted by 'un fantassin de la ligne en petite tenue' who
has planted himself in his path, congratulating him and calling him
'colonel'. This turns out to be Hussonet in fancy dress (pp. 49–50).
It is also specified that the dispersal of Hussonet's talents in all
directions is linguistic: 'Hussonnet ne fut pas drôle. A force d'écrire
quotidiennement sur toute sorte de sujets, de lire beaucoup de jour-
neaux, d'entendre beaucoup de discussions et d'émettre des paradoxes
pour éblouir, il avait fini par perdre la notion exacte des choses,
s'aveuglant lui-même avec ses faibles pétards' (p. 84).

Frédéric is described as coming to resemble Arnoux more and
more, and undoubtedly Arnoux is the character who most consistently
leads Frédéric in the direction of dissipation and moral decline.
Frédéric's first visit to the *Art industriel* is an introduction to Arnoux's
typical environment: the rooms are packed, nobody can move or
breathe amidst the cigar smoke and dazzling light, and all is bustle
and activity against a background of different conversations. This
moral chaos is carried over into the description of the evening at the
Alhambra, where even the talkative Arnoux is outdone:

Mais ses paroles étaient couvertes par le tapage de la musique; et, sitôt le
quadrille ou la polka terminés, tous s'abattaient sur les tables, appelaient le
garçon, riaient; les bouteilles de bière et de limonade gazeuse détonaient dans
les feuillages, des femmes criaient comme des poules; quelquefois, deux
messieurs voulaient se battre; un voleur fut arrêté.   (p. 35)

It is Arnoux who takes Frédéric to Rosanette's ball, a fancy-dress
party-cum-orgy clearly intended to symbolize the superficial pleasures
of a diffuse and essentially worthless experience which is again, at
one point, quite specifically related to language:

Une horloge allemande, munie d'un coq, carillonnant deux heures, provoqua
sur le coucou force plaisanteries. Toutes sortes de propos s'ensuivirent:
calembours, anecdotes, vantardises, gageures, mensonges tenus pour vrais,
assertions improbables, un tumulte de paroles qui bientôt s'éparpilla en
conversations particulières.   (p. 53)

When the whole party collapses in exhaustion, it is appropriately a
moment of sudden silence which shows up the real value of the ball,

ns a window and daylight transforms the scene: 'Il
nation d'étonnement, puis un silence' (p. 54). The
wers are all wilting, there are drink stains everywhere,
collapsed and make-up runs down perspiring faces.
itement is no more than a sordid chaos, and Frédéric
fails, in his half-drunken stupor, to recognize the
'deux grands yeux noirs' which were not, of course, anything to do
with the ball.

The clearest reinstatement of an inarticulate character in any of
Flaubert's works takes place in *Un Cœur simple*. If the problem of
irony in this story can be put aside for the time being, it is clear at
least that the straightforward linear plot raises a completely illiterate
and ineloquent servant to the position of central character and main
focus of interest. She is quite uneducated apart from Paul's explanations of a picture book geography, where she speaks directly, as in
the bull incident, it is in very short sentences, and she is so silent and
orderly that she seems to function automatically. Her life is made up
of regular work and devoted service, her fondness for those around
her is constantly shown in small acts of kindness, and her reaction
to the grief of Victor's death leads her to contain her sorrow and keep
on working. Though she starts out with a certain amount of common
sense (her suspicion of Théodore's promises, her dealings with Mme
Aubain's tenant farmers and visitors), as the story progresses she
appears more and more stupid.

The chief foil for Félicité is M. Bourais, the pedantic culmination
of Flaubert's long line of self-satisfied 'knowledgeable' characters,
whom Mme Aubain regards as an authority to consult on all important matters (on the bathing at Trouville, on the choice of a school
for Paul). Flaubert completes the undermining of such characters by
making Bourais a cheap villain who is finally exposed, a disgracing
of 'intelligence' all the greater in that it is the parrot Loulou (a
caricature of Félicité in his relations with language), who is given the
privilege of seeing through him from the start, laughing at him every
time he sees him and humiliating him to such an extent that Bourais
has to arrive at Mme Aubain's by stealth (with his hat covering his
face). The contrast between Félicité and Bourais is underlined when
she asks him to show her where Victor is on the map. Bourais,
wrapped up in lengthy explanations of longitudes and so on, is
enormously amused when asked to point out Victor's house: 'et il
avait un beau sourire de cuistre devant l'ahurissement de Félicité [...]
Bourais leva les bras, il éternua, rit énormément; une candeur pareille
excitait sa joie; et Félicité n'en comprenait pas le motif, elle qui

s'attendait peut-être à voir jusqu'au portrait de son neveu, tant son intelligence était bornée!' (p. 171).[7] But Flaubert makes plain the relative values of their different versions of 'understanding'. Félicité does not need Bourais's intellectual approach to the world; indeed it is *because* of her ignorance that she is able to follow Victor in her imagination. She is thirsty on his behalf when it is hot, frightened for him when there is a storm, and her simplicity is enhanced by a genuine interest: her attempts to visualize Havana involve clouds of tobacco 'à cause des cigares' (p. 171.)

Félicité's heart and imagination dominate her whole conception of reality; for example because Virginie and Victor are linked in her heart she imagines that their destiny must be the same. Similarly her understanding of religion takes place on the level of imagination and emotion, as she reduces Christian imagery to her own surroundings:

Les semailles, les moissons, les pressoirs, toutes ces choses familières dont parle l'Évangile, se trouvaient dans sa vie; le passage de Dieu les avait sanctifiées; et elle aima plus tendrement les agneaux par amour de l'Agneau, les colombes à cause du Saint-Esprit [...] C'est peut-être sa lumière qui voltige la nuit aux bords des marécages, son haleine qui pousse les nuées, sa voix qui rend les cloches harmonieuses; et elle demeurait dans une adoration, jouissant de la fraîcheur des murs et de la tranquillité de l'église. (p. 170)

When the priest tells stories from the Bible she can vividly imagine Paradise and the Great Flood, and 'pleura en écoutant la Passion'. But when it comes to dogma: 'elle n'y comprenait rien, ne tâcha même pas de comprendre' (p. 170). Her sympathetic understanding is such that she can forgive Mme Aubain for sending Virginie away to the convent, and for thinking her daughter so much more important than Victor. The height of this power comes at the moment of Virginie's First Communion when Félicité identifies with Virginie so closely that she feels she has become her: 'avec l'imagination que donnent les vraies tendresses, il lui sembla qu'elle était elle-même cette enfant' (p. 170).[8] Her qualities are those which Flaubert elsewhere attributes to the artist. Like Justin's her love can transform the ugliest of realities: she forms a fetishistic attachment to Virginie's hat although it has been eaten away by vermin, loves the stuffed Loulou all the more and kisses him farewell regardless of his worm-eaten state, and devotedly tends the cancer-ridden Père Colmiche. Certainly Emma Bovary could not have accepted and pitied the blind beggar, and the importance of this particular theme is shown by the fact that, in *La Légende de Saint Julien l'Hospitalier*, Julien's accession to sainthood seems ultimately to be dependent on his willing and selfless embrace of the leper. The enormous effort over self required by Julien sets in full relief Félicité's entirely spontaneous selflessness, which is quite without personal motive. While her 'sainthood' emerges largely through association with the saints of the other stories of the *Trois Contes*, Flaubert would evidently consider it deserved: though (or because) an inarticulate servant cut off from the world, she is rewarded with an experience that is the richer and the more complete for being imaginary.

3

BY-PASSING SPE

Sartre's masterly account of Flaubert's linguistic adventure shows that an uneasy relationship with words and meaning, pathological in terms of personal biography,[1] had an original and positive function in the creation of an aesthetic — a conception of art that seeks to maintain language as an opaque and autonomous order. It is the extraordinary convergence of recent critical views upon this particular perception of Flaubert that has elevated him to a position as precursor of a now especially prized way of writing. Gérard Genette, for example, characterizing Flaubert's mature prose by its deliberate refusal of eloquence, attributes to him a 'projet de *ne rien dire*' which could be seen as informing one whole movement within modern literature (1963, p. 57).[2] If language should ideally be sensed as opaque, then characters with linguistic difficulties, who permanently sense its opaqueness, have an advantage from an aesthetic point of view. If Flaubert's writing is based on a refusal of eloquence, then fictional characters who lack eloquence deserve an evaluation that takes account of their part in the production of that writing. Is it then possible that all those useless inarticulate characters should take a share in Flaubert's personal triumph, that the likes of Charles and Félicité helped to forge the direction of modern literature?

The parrot Loulou, a rather special inarticulate character, might well stand as an emblem for Flaubert's handling of language. Endlessly repeating his famous set of (for him) contentless phrases, he represents the autonomy of language, emphasized by Flaubert himself in his digression on the man who works the telegraph in *Par les Champs et par les grèves*:

Quelle drôle de vie que celle de l'homme qui reste là, dans cette petite cabane à faire mouvoir ces deux perches et à tirer sur ces ficelles; rouage inintelligent d'une machine muette pour lui, il peut mourir sans connaître un seul des événements qu'il a appris, un seul mot de tous ceux qu'il aura dits [...] Un peu plus, un peu moins, ne sommes-nous pas tous comme ce brave homme, *parlant des mots qu'on nous a appris et que nous apprenons sans les comprendre.*

(II, p. 484, my emphasis)

Giacomo (*Bibliomanie*), on a Sunday walk through the town, language is quite literally experienced as a baffling string of noises:

Il ramassa dans la route quelques bribes de phrases, quelques mots, quelques cris, mais il lui semblait que c'était toujours le même son, la même voix, c'était un brouhaha vague, confus, une musique bizarre et bruyante qui bourdonnait dans son cerveau et l'accablait. (I, p. 81)

The experience of listening to any language is often conveyed in a confused and fragmented way. At the *Comices agricoles* M. Lieuvain's voice 'vous arrivait par lambeaux de phrases' (I, p. 624), and a gathering at the Dambreuses's is perceived by Frédéric as so many disjointed phrases: '— Ah bah! — Eh! eh!' (II, p. 66). Frédéric extracts nothing from his law lectures but the monotonous sound of the lecturer's voice (p. 15), and is frustrated by the ridiculous Spaniard at the *Club de l'Intelligence*. However, he sometimes chooses to spend an hour listening to a Chinese lesson at the Collège de France, in which he is outdone by Bouvard and Pécuchet who attent an Arabic class at the same establishment: 'et le professeur fut étonné de voir cex deux inconnus qui tâchaient de prendre des notes' (II, p. 204). Flaubert has deliberately chosen languages strange to the French ear, and that a corresponding pleasure can be gained from cultivating the opaqueness of any language is spelled out in a letter to Alfred le Poittevin:[3]

je m'étonne parfois d'entendre dire les choses les plus naturelles et les plus simples. Le mot le plus banal *me tient parfois en singulière admiration*. Il y a des gestes, des sons de voix dont je ne reviens pas, et des niaiseries *qui me donnent presque le vertige*. As-tu quelquefois *écouté attentivement* des gens qui parlaient une langue étrangère que tu n'entendais pas? J'en suis là. (*Corr.* (B) I, p. 252 (1845), my emphases)

Not surprisingly Sartre uses this quotation as an example of the aesthetic attitude to language (*L'Idiot* II, p. 1976); moreover it already incorporates the sort of qualities associated later with the ideal experience of the work of art (astonishment, admiration and giddiness).

When Mme Arnoux, showing Frédéric around the factory, uses the ugly word 'patouillards' to explain a piece of machinery, he is shocked and finds it somehow wrong (II, p. 79). The fact that the content is correct, that it is specifying a meaning, does not come into consideration. Indeed, when Mélie listens to Bouvard and Pécuchet's play readings, it is her lack of comprehension which largely creates her enjoyment: 'La petite bonne s'amusait sans y rien comprendre, ébahie du langage, fascinée par le ronron des vers' (II, p. 246). The would-be actors presumably appreciate this, for their chief concern is with training their voices, and, lying on their beds in their separate rooms, they simultaneously follow exercises to increase their vocal range and subtlety. The way they play with an echo, accidentally produced by their attempts at garden landscaping, indicates the aesthetic pleasure to be obtained by playing with sounds. When they decide to write a play Flaubert makes them unable to think up a subject, and they would clearly do better to follow their natural inclination to enjoy the material qualities of language. As Bernheimer illustrates in his excellent analysis of the fruit-growing episode (1974, pp. 144–5), their liking for strange words is the primary cause of the disaster, and while pointing this out Flaubert creates a verbal effect for the reader through his ironic repetition of the fantastic names which had beguiled them: 'Les passe-colmars étaient perdus, comme le bési-des-véterans et les triomphes-de-jordoigne. À peine s'il restait parmi les pommes quelques bons-papas; et douze tétons-de-Vénus' (II, p. 214). Similarly, while deflating the 'symbolic' approach adopted in their historical study of the duc d'Angoulême (an imbecile), Flaubert achieves an effect from the repetition of the word 'pont' which quite destroys its interpretative usefulness:

On doit y relever l'importance qu'eurent les ponts. D'abord, il s'expose inutilement sur le pont de l'Inn; il enlève le pont Saint Esprit et le pont de Lauriol; à Lyon, les deux ponts lui sont funestes, et sa fortune expire devant le pont de Sèvres.   (p. 241)

Needless to say, their historical research was in any case dominated by an interest in 'tous ceux dont les noms étaient bizarres ou agréables' (p. 240). The 'tout devint phallus' episode, in which they gather together a collection of chair legs, old bolts, etc. and ask visitors 'À quoi trouvez-vous que cela ressemble?' (p. 237), clearly deflates the idea of a motivated symbol, and when they invent their own mnemonic system based on their house and garden, they might be congratulated for assimilating reality itself into a totally arbitrary system of signs, which, since they forget what everything stands for, is certainly non-referential:

Pour plus de clarté, ils prirent comme base mnémotechnique leur propre maison, leur domicile, attachant à chacune de ses parties un fait distinct, et la cour, le jardin, les environs, tout le pays n'avaient plus d'autre sens que de faciliter la mémoire. Les bornages dans la campagne limitaient certaines époques, les pommiers étaient des arbres généalogiques, les buissons des batailles, le monde devenait symbole. Ils cherchaient sur les murs des quantités de choses absentes, finissaient par les voir, mais ne savaient plus les dates qu'elles représentaient.   (p. 240)

43

The finest excuse for playing with the 'signifier' is the experiment in spiritualism, when they try to get in touch with Bouvard's dead father:

Pécuchet, bien vite, souffla les mots, notés sur un carton.

— Ischyros, Athanatos, Adonaï, Sadaï, Eloy, Messiasos (la kyrielle était longue), je te conjure, je t'observe, je t'ordonne, ô Béchet!

Puis, baissant la voix:

— Où es-tu, Béchet? Béchet! Béchet! Béchet! (p. 268)

This evident corruption of the names Bouvard and Pécuchet is produced in the story by the characters themselves, as is their invention of 'la Bouvarine', a new liqueur: 'Car il fallait un nom facile à retenir et pourtant bizarre. Ayant longtemps cherché, ils décidèrent qu'elle se nommerait la "Bouvarine"' (pp. 218–19). When they turn to teaching Flaubert ignores the content of their lessons to foreground the sound of the symphonic performance: 'Les maîtres professaient à la même heure, dans leurs chambres respectives, et, la cloison étant mince, ces quatre voix, une flûtée, une profonde et deux aiguës, composaient un charivari abominable' (p. 289). It is Bouvard and Pécuchet's attempts to apply language to the practical world that cause their chain of failures, each experiment based on a different set of reference books (usually recommended by the pedant Dumouchel). After their long exploration of Homais's dictum 'Croyez-vous qu'il faille, pour être agronome, avoir soi-même labouré la terre ou engraissés des volailles?' (I, p. 619), their return to indiscriminate copying could be seen as a sort of aesthetic wisdom. Since their *copie* was to form the second volume of the novel, the behaviour of Bouvard and Pécuchet is deeply implicated in Flaubert's total conception of the work.[4]

My claim is, however, that in a generally less grotesque manner, characters throughout Flaubert's work are busily involved in foregrounding the material qualities of language. It is Charles's extreme inarticulacy which creates the famous 'Charbovari', and the joyful and noisy scene to which it gives rise:

Le *nouveau*, prenant alors une résolution extrême, ouvrit une bouche démesurée et lança, à pleins poumons, comme pour appeler quelqu'un, ce mot: *Charbovari*.

Ce fut un vacarme qui s'élança d'un bond, monta en *crescendo*, avec des éclats de voix aigus (on hurlait, on aboyait, on trépignait, on répétait: *Charbovari! Charbovari!*) puis qui roula en notes isolées, se calmant à grand'peine, et parfois qui reprenait tout à coup sur la ligne d'un banc où saillissait encore, çà et là, comme un pétard mal éteint, quelque rire étouffé.

(I, p. 575)

Charles's aesthetic role is less apparent than Bouvard and Pécuchet's only because of the more traditionally representational form of the novel, which makes him operate as a fictional but convincing 'real person'. When he falls in love he is enchanted by Emma's voice, but does not get as far as the meaning of what she is saying: 'Charles reprit une à une les phrases qu'elle avait dites, tâchant de se les rappeler, d'en compléter le sens' (p. 582). At the opera in Rouen he cannot follow what is going on: 'Il avouait, du reste, ne pas comprendre l'histoire − à cause de la musique, qui nuisait beaucoup aux paroles' (p. 650). That an important aesthetic issue is at stake here is underlined by the fact that Emma can follow the plot and is described as liking the music at school for the content of the songs. For Flaubert is careful to point out that she is 'de tempérament plus sentimentale qu'artiste' (p. 586), unlike Mme Renaud, in the first *Éducation*, as she listens to Henry: 'Quand il parlait, elle se taisait et écoutait le son de sa voix, comme on écoute chanter, sans chercher le sens des mots quand la musique est belle' (I, p. 330).

In other words Flaubert builds up an enjoyment of the precedence of sound over meaning, and often it is the erotic fascination of a loved person's voice which makes meaning irrelevant: 'Maria se mit à parler. Je ne sais ce qu'elle dit, je me laissais enchanter par le son de ses paroles' (I, p. 238). When Maria describes her tastes in art we are not told what she says, but only the way in which she says it: 'elle avait des mots simples et expressifs qui partaient en relief, et surtout avec tant de négligé et de grâce, tant d'abandon, de nonchalance, que vous auriez dit qu'elle chantait' (p. 238). The narrator's lasting memory of Maria is tied up with her beautiful voice, and with the magnetic fascination which it exerts: 'voix douce et pure, qui vous enivre et qui vous fait mourir d'amour, voix qui a un corps, tant elle est belle, et qui séduit, comme s'il y avait un charme à ses mots' (p. 236). Indeed Flaubert himself will increasingly use the physical qualities of prose to induce the same ecstasy that he himself felt before certain words or sentences: 'des phrases me font pâmer' (*Corr.* (C) VII, p. 281 (1875)), 'des phrases qui me ravissent' (*Corr.* (C) VII, p. 294 (1876)), of which the following are obviously examples:

Je donnerais toutes les légendes de Gavarni pour certaines expressions et coupes de maîtres comme 'l'ombre était nuptiale, auguste et solennelle' de Victor Hugo, ou ceci du président de Montesquieu: 'Les vices d'Alexandre étaient extrêmes comme ses vertus. Il était terrible dans sa colère. Elle le rendait cruel.'   (*Corr.* (C) VII, p. 282 (1875))

The latter 'gem' is surely the model for Flaubert's own extensive use of the 'coupe', especially the tripartite asyndeton, for example: 'On avait reconnu Iaokanann. Son nom circulait. D'autres accoururent' (II, p. 193). Flaubert's metaphorically erotic vocabulary (*pâmer, ravir,* etc.),[5] suggests that he is close to exemplifying Roland Barthes's now well-known notion of textual pleasure, where equating 'plaisir' with contentment and 'jouissance' with 'évanouissement' (and regretting that there is no French word to cover both), he asks: 'Qu'est-ce que la signifiance? C'est le sens *en ce qu'il est produit sensuellement'* (1975, p. 97). This resembles the death of meaning which Sartre and Genette attribute to Flaubert's mature prose, and it is strange that Barthes, who closes *Le Plaisir du texte* with a discussion of the voice and the audio-visual, does not think to refer to Flaubert, who in 1853 speaks of both 'la physiologie du style' (*Corr.* (B) II, p. 445) and 'l'anatomie du style' (p. 427). How close to Flaubert Barthes is when he writes:

S'il était possible d'imaginer une esthétique du plaisir textuel, il faudrait y inclure: *l'écriture à haute voix.* Cette écriture vocale (qui n'est pas du tout la parole), on ne la pratique pas, mais c'est sans doute elle que recommandait Artaud et que demande Sollers. Parlons-en comme si elle existait [...] Eu égard aux sons de la langue, *l'écriture à haute voix* n'est pas phonologique, mais phonétique; son objectif n'est pas la clarté des messages, le théâtre des émotions; ce qu'elle cherche (dans une perspective de jouissance), ce sont les incidents pulsionnels, c'est le langage tapissé de peau, un texte où l'on puisse entendre le grain du gosier, la patine des consonnes, la volupté des voyelles, toute une stéréophonie de la chair profonde: l'articulation du corps, de la langue, non celle du sens, du langage. (1975, pp. 104–5)

For Flaubert's insistence upon reading his sentences aloud to himself as he writes them ('gueuler des phrases') is much more than a stylist's quirk, and the supreme moment for Flaubert as artist was never so much publication as reading his works to his friends.[6]

In Flaubert's stories words fascinate as physical objects in their own right, to the extent that they are materialized by the person seduced by them, and can be seen coming out of the speaker's mouth:

Chaque mot qui sortait de sa bouche semblait à Frédéric être une chose nouvelle, une dépendance exclusive de sa personne. (II, pp. 25–6)

Je l'avais écouté avec avidité, j'avais regardé tous les mots sortir de sa bouche. (I, p. 268)

Je regardais les mots qui sortait de ta bouche, je te considérais avec étonnement. (I, p. 295)

Frédéric makes quite explicit the transference of the eroti
person to word: 'et les délices de la chair et de l'âme étai
pour moi dans votre nom que je me répétais, en tâcha
sur mes lèvres' (II, p. 161). Since the content of conve
frequently undermined when there is a sexual attractio
participants, the fact that they exchange clichés ceases to ～～ ～ ～ ～ ～ ～ ～
This is evident in the early conversations of Henry and Mme Renaud
in the first *Éducation*, where contact is established by platitudes: 'car
ils étaient déjà un peu amis, non par ce qu'ils s'étaient dit, mais par
le ton dont ils se l'étaient dit' (I, p. 284). There is an exact parallel
in *Madame Bovary*: Emma and Léon's commonplace conversation
on sunsets and reading by the fire is heavily satirized, but it is made
clear at the same time both that a genuine communication is taking
place and that the words used are not significant: 'une de ces vagues
conversations où le hasard des phrases vous ramène toujours au centre
fixe d'une sympathie commune' (I, pp. 602–3). But nowhere is the
irrelevance of content in an intimate conversation so vividly underlined as in Félicité's endless 'exchanges' with her parrot: 'Ils avaient
des dialogues, lui, débitant à satiété les trois phrases de son répertoire,
et elle, y répondant par des mots sans plus de suite, mais où son cœur
s'épanchait' (II, p. 175).

When Emma and Léon return from a visit to her baby, 'les paroles
qu'ils se disaient' function only as sounds in a poetic juxtaposition
with the rhythm of their footsteps and the rustling of Emma's dress
(I, p. 606). And when, a few lines later, an example of their trivial
conversation is provided, the narrator comments on the inner quality
of their communication: 'N'avaient-ils pas autre chose à se dire? Leurs
yeux pourtant étaient pleins d'une causerie plus sérieuse; et, tandis
qu'ils s'efforçaient à trouver des phrases banales, ils sentaient une
même langueur les envahir tous les deux; c'était comme un murmure de
l'âme, profond, continu, qui dominait celui des voix' (p. 606). During
the unexpected meeting in the street of Frédéric and Mme Arnoux, a
moment of complete silence and a poetic description of Mme Arnoux
standing in the sunlight are followed by a few remarks to each other
on the family and the weather before the two characters go their
separate ways. Yet Frédéric, we are told, would not have exchanged
this uneventful encounter for the most beautiful of adventures:

Une suavité infinie s'épanchait de ses beaux yeux; et, balbutiant au hasard,
les premières paroles venues:
— Comment se porte Arnoux? dit Frédéric.
— Je vous remercie!
— Et vos enfants?

— Ils vont très bien!

— Ah!... ah! – Quel beau temps nous avons, n'est-ce pas?

— Magnifique c'est vrai!

— Vous faites des courses?

— Oui.

Et avec une lente inclination de tête:

— Adieu!

Elle ne lui avait pas tendu la main, n'avait pas dit un seul mot affectueux, ne l'avait même pas invité à venir chez elle, n'importe! il n'eût point donné cette rencontre pour la plus belle des aventures; et il en ruminait la douceur tout en continuant sa route. (II, pp. 102–3)

This passage contains a specific hint that such moments could be more important to the novel than events that forward the action, and provides a fine example of how silence, or even clichés where the meaning is virtually non-existent, can be as emotion-laden as any eloquent speech.

Perhaps the clearest example of the constant rejection of speech in Flaubert's works is Narr'Havas's courtship of Salammbô, an unusual pastoral moment in the novel. Narr'Havas, we are told, 'se mit à raconter la campagne'. But instead of following his story the narrative immediately dissolves into a description of the garden. Finally Narr'Havas arrives at his declaration of love and at clichés:

Mais Narr'Havas, poursuivant, compara ses désirs à des fleurs qui languissent après la pluie, à des voyageurs perdus qui attendent le jour. Il lui dit encore qu'elle était plus belle que la lune, meilleure que le vent du matin et que le visage de l'hôte. Il ferait venir pour elle, du pays des Noirs, des choses comme il n'y en avait pas à Carthage, et les appartements de leur maison seraient sablés avec de la poudre d'or.

Le soir tombait, des senteurs de baume s'exhalaient. Pendant longtemps, ils se regardèrent en silence, et les yeux de Salammbô, au fond de ses longues draperies, avaient l'air de deux étoiles dans l'ouverture d'un nuage. Avant que le soleil fût couché, il se retira. (I, 788–9)

These are the very moments analysed by Genette as moments of silence in the story coinciding with the novel's own dissolution into silence:

Moments [...] doublement silencieux: parce que les personnages ont cessé de parler pour se mettre à l'écoute du monde et de leur rêve, parce que cette interruption du dialogue et de l'action suspend la parole même du roman et l'absorbe, pour un temps, dans une sorte d'interrogation sans voix [...] ces instants musicaux où le récit se perd et s'oublie dans l'extase d'une contemplation infinie. (1966(b), pp. 237–8)

By-passing speech

These silent moments run right through Flaubert's works. Often preceded by short exchanges of banal conversation, they show up, by contrast, the relative poverty of speech as an instrument of expression and communication. Inarticulate characters are in the best position to bring about these wordless moments of bliss, and, since such passages have an aesthetic function in the novels themselves, by a circular movement the characters themselves contribute to the downgrading of language which founds their own value.

Paradoxically, given Henry's later development into a smooth-talking man of the world, his love affair with Mme Renaud is the first thorough exploration in Flaubert's works of a relationship which places value on silence:

> Mais les plus doux moments étaient ceux où, ayant épuisé toute parole humaine et se taisant, ils se regardaient avec des yeux avides, puis ils baissaient la tête et, absorbés, songeaient à tout ce qui ne se dit pas. (I, p. 292)

> ils ne se parlaient pas, mais, les bras passés autour de la taille, ils se serraient étroitement l'un contre l'autre; on eût dit que, sans le secours de la parole, ils voulaient se faire passer dans le cœur l'un l'autre leurs souvenirs communs, leurs espérances faites à deux, leurs vagues angoisses, leurs regrets, leurs inquiétudes peut-être, et mettre tout cela à l'unisson. (p. 332)

In *Madame Bovary*, the persistent attack on the easy and worthless 'eloquence' of such characters as Homais sets in relief a positive proliferation of expressive silences, which punctuate all three love relationships. Charles's early meetings with Emma often dissolve into a silence during which the first real contact is established:

> On s'était dit adieu, on ne parlait plus; le grand air l'entourait, levant pêle-mêle les petits cheveux follets de sa nuque, ou secouant sur sa hanche les cordons de son tablier, qui se tortillaient comme des banderoles. Une fois, par un temps de dégel, l'écorce des arbres suintait dans la cour, la neige sur les couvertures des bâtiments se fondait. Elle était sur le seuil; elle alla chercher son ombrelle, elle l'ouvrit. L'ombrelle, de soie gorge-de-pigeon, que traversait le soleil, éclairait de reflets mobiles la peau blanche de sa figure. Elle souriait là-dessous à la chaleur tiède; et on entendait les gouttes d'eau, une à une, tomber sur la moire tendue. (I, p. 580)

At the moment of Léon's departure from Yonville: 'il y eut un silence. Ils se regardèrent; et leurs pensées, confondues dans la même angoisse, s'étreignaient étroitement, comme deux poitrines palpitantes' (p. 614). The superiority of silence over speech is often suggested: 'La conversation fut languissante, madame Bovary l'abandonnant à chaque minute, tandis qu'il demeurait lui-même comme tout embarrassé [...]

Elle ne parlait pas; il se taisait, captivé par son silence comme il l'eût été de ses paroles' (p. 609). The emotion and lyricism of one of Emma and Léon's best moments, the evening on the water during their 'honeymoon' at Rouen, is also characterized by silence:

> La barque suivait le bord des îles. Ils restaient au fond, tous les deux cachés par l'ombre, sans parler. Les avirons carrés sonnaient entre les tolets de fer; et cela marquait dans le silence comme un battement de métronome, tandis qu'à l'arrière la bauce qui traînait ne discontinuait pas son petit clapotement doux dans l'eau. (p. 661)

The intervention of tiny sounds intensifies the silence, always presented as something positive rather than just an absence of noise, and the last evening that Emma spends with Rodolphe (by the river at the bottom of her garden) is a fine example of the poetic power of this particular effect:

> Ils ne se parlaient pas, trop perdus qu'ils étaient dans l'envahissement de leur rêverie. La tendresse des anciens jours leur revenait au cœur, abondante et silencieuse comme la rivière qui coulait, avec autant de mollesse qu'en apportait le parfum des seringas, et projetait dans leurs souvenirs des ombres plus démesurées et plus mélancoliques que celles des saules immobiles qui s'allongeaient sur l'herbe. Souvent quelque bête nocturne, hérisson ou belette, se mettant en chasse, dérangeait les feuilles, ou bien on entendait par moments une pêche mure qui tombait toute seule de l'espalier. (p. 641)

As might be expected, Frédéric's relationship with Mme Arnoux is most fully consummated by still and expressive silences: 'Mme Arnoux tourna son beau visage, en lui tendant la main, et ils fermèrent les yeux, absorbés dans une ivresse qui était comme un bercement doux et infini. Puis ils restèrent à se contempler, face à face, l'un près de l'autre' (II, p. 138). But the four principal women of *L'Éducation sentimentale* all share in these moments, as where Frédéric and Louise walk through the sand by the river at Nogent, or where even Mme Dambreuse's seduction is followed by 'une suspension universelle des choses' (p. 141). However the most memorable of these passages is probably the Fontainebleau episode with Rosanette. Rosanette is much more than a simple foil for Mme Arnoux (the 'grand amour' versus the 'amour joyeux et facile' (p. 138)), for she is the product of subtle characterization in her own right. In the tour of the palace she has just proved her complete ignorance and lack of culture, and clearly she prefers the carp and the souvenir stall selling wood carvings to the beauty of the palace and the forest. Yet she is allowed one of the most intense moments of the novel. For, although Frédéric's very presence at Fontainebleau during the June Days might invite an ironic

reading, the pages of lyrical description of the
presented seriously, and the whole burden of ex
passed to the natural surroundings. The forest is
in silence, intensified only by an occasional sound
'Quand la voiture s'arrêtait, il se faisait un sile
ment on entendait le souffle du cheval dans les br
cri d'oiseau très faible répété' (p. 126). Rosanette, for
becomes almost a part of the forest. At times they lie on the grass,
gazing at each other in silence, at another Rosanette for the first time
gives some difficult details of her early life, less significant in themselves than the will to speak about herself and the suggestion of inex-
pressible emotion. As her story breaks off at the crucial point:

Les feuilles autour d'eux susurraient, dans un fouillis d'herbes une grande
digitale se balançait, la lumière coulait comme une onde sur le gazon; et le
silence était coupé à intervalles rapides par le broutement de la vache qu'on
ne voyait plus.   (p. 128)

The narrator concludes this passage with a general remark on the
poverty of verbal expression: 'il est difficile d'exprimer exactement
quoi que ce soit; aussi les unions complètes sont rares' (p. 129). But
here the lyrical description of nature − especially of the trees and
rocks of the forest that seem to move and to come alive with human
and animal qualities − takes over from Rosanette's ineloquence.

At the time of Emma's first depressions nature takes a sinister turn,
and her melancholy and boredom are later conveyed via a howling
dog and a monotonous distant chiming. Allowing particularly
momentous occasions to have their reverberations in nature is a
literary commonplace, of course. But whereas in Shakespeare recourse
to nature might be symbolic (for example the storm in *King Lear*),
or used to underline the universality of events, Flaubert uses versions
of the pathetic fallacy in a rather special way, namely to 'help' his
inarticulate characters by giving to poetic description of surroundings
the task of conveying emotion. In *Un Cœur simple*, when Félicité goes
off to work enveloped in silent grief for Victor's death: 'les prairies
étaient vides' (II, p. 172). (When she had tried to verbalize her suffering, 'Pauvre petit gars!' was all she could manage.) In the first
Éducation, the pieces of furniture in Henry's room become 'ces muets
témoins de leur bonheur' (I, p. 322), and on the last morning before
their elopement it becomes apparent that Henry's happiness with Mme
Renaud has been associated with their surroundings:

il marcha encore une fois à toutes les diverses places où, à des jours différents,
il avait marché, rêvé, aimé. Il entra aussi dans le cabinet de M. Renaud,

sur les chaises, sur les fauteuils, regarda le titre des livres; il visita tous
s appartements, il erra dans les corridors et dans l'escalier; en contemplant
cette nature inerte et pourtant expressive par les souvenirs qui s'en exhalaient,
il se demandait comment il ferait pour s'en détacher, et si elle ne participait
pas à la substance même de son cœur. (p. 331)

Particular objects can take on human qualities. When Frédéric waits
in vain for Mme Arnoux: 'Les objets les plus minimes devenaient pour
lui des compagnons, ou plutôt des spectateurs ironiques; et les façades
régulières des maisons lui semblaient impitoyables' (II, p. 109), while
Mme Arnoux's personal trinkets, viewed through Frédéric's eyes, are
'presque animés comme des personnes' (p. 28). In *Un Cœur simple*,
Félicité and Mme Aubain, who have never been close to each other,
are brought together by their discovery of Virginie's plush hat:

> Elles retrouvèrent un petit chapeau de peluche, à longs poils, couleur marron;
> mais il était tout mangé de vermine. Félicité le réclama pour elle-même. Leurs
> yeux se fixèrent l'une sur l'autre, s'emplirent de larmes; enfin la maîtresse
> ouvrit ses bras, la servante s'y jeta; et elles s'étreignirent, satisfaisant leur
> douleur dans un baiser qui les égalisait.
> C'était la première fois de leur vie, Mme Aubain n'étant pas d'une nature
> expansive. (II, p. 173)

Thus fetishism, which would be defined as a pathological relationship
to objects, could be seen to have a more positive function in Flaubert's
works, in that it can improve the quality of human relationships for
his inarticulate characters.

A final and important means of communication which is often
given precedence over spoken language has already appeared in many
of the quotations in this chapter. In the very early story *Un Parfum
à sentir*, when Pedrillo returns from gambling away his last money,
Marguerite's sympathetic power of understanding removes the need
for words:

> elle comprit la sueur qui coula de son visage; elle vit pourquoi ses yeux étaient
> rongés de colère, elle devina les choses qu'il pensait, à travers la pâleur de
> son front, et elle savait ce que voulaient dire ses claquements de dents.
> Ils restèrent tous deux ainsi, sans rien dire, sans se communiquer ni leurs
> peines ni leur désespoir, mais leurs yeux pourtant avaient parlé et s'étaient
> dit des pensées tristes et déchirantes. (I, p. 61)

Similarly, it is Mâtho's eyes which are finally able to convey his
feelings to Salammbô; 'ces effroyables prunelles la contemplaient, et
la conscience lui surgit de tout ce qu'il avait souffert pour elle' (I,
p. 796). Even Charles is given a brief moment of victory over
Rodolphe, in the specific form of a look powerful enough to kill

speech: 'il y eut même un instant où Charles, plein d'une fureur sombre, fixa ses yeux contre Rodolphe, qui, dans une sorte d'effroi, s'interrompit' (I, p. 692). It is difficult to imagine such a power extended to one of Flaubert's complacent and talkative characters – indeed the most powerful 'judging' gazes are given to the *corpse* of Julien's father and to that of M. Dambreuse: 'Ses paupières s'étaient rouvertes; et les pupilles, bien que noyées dans des ténèbres visqueuses, avaient une expression énigmatique, intolérable. Frédéric croyait y voir comme un jugement porté sur lui' (II, p. 145).

What might be seen in the first instance as a simple love language of the eyes – 'nous restâmes longtemps nous regardant sans rien dire' (I, p. 259) – induces, in *Novembre*, an almost oppressive fascination: 'voulant secouer cette fascination qui m'endormait [...] ses yeux brillaient, m'enflammaient, son regard m'enveloppait plus que ses bras, j'étais perdu dans son œil'. Marie's eye becomes a dilating pupil, exercising a magnetic, trance-like attraction: 'chaque effluve de ce regard béant, semblable aux cercles successifs que décrit l'orfraie, m'attachait de plus en plus à cette magie terrible' (p. 261). In the first *Éducation*, Mme Renaud's hypnotic gaze plays a quite literal role in the seduction of Henry: 'Toute la journée elle m'avait regardé de façon étrange, et moi-même je ne pouvais quitter son regard, qui m'entourait comme un cercle dans lequel je vivais' (I, p. 311). This general atmosphere of soporific amazement sets up a 'béance' and an 'ébahissement' typical of their affair: 'Ils se regardaient, avides et stupéfaits' (p. 314); 'elle le contemplait avec des yeux fixes, enflammés comme des flambeaux' (p. 315), which is carried into the relationship between Emma and Léon: 'Ils ne se parlaient plus; mais ils sentaient, en se regardant, un bruissement dans leurs têtes, comme si quelque chose de sonore se fut réciproquement échappé de leurs prunelles fixes' (I, p. 654).

Of course Rodolphe's 'on se devine!' (p. 623) and his town-hall patter on mesmerism might seem to undermine the seriousness of this absolutely typical communion between lovers. Indeed nowhere is mesmerism more fiercely satirized than in Bouvard and Pécuchet's flirtation with hypnosis, for example their unlikely cure of the swollen cow:

Ayant retroussé leurs manches, ils se placèrent l'un devant les cornes, l'autre à la croupe, et, avec de grands efforts intérieurs et une gesticulation frénétique, ils écartaient les doigts pour répandre sur l'animal des ruisseaux de fluide, tandis que le fermier, son épouse, leur garçon et des voisins les regardaient presque effrayés.

(II, p. 265)

But Flaubert always parodies his methods at some stage, and the terror felt by the audience here is not unrelated to the desired effect of Flaubert's fictions. That the material and fluid quality of hypnotic contemplation should be a central part of Jules's famous encounter with the mangy dog, suggests that Flaubert's artistic aims are seriously at stake. Clearly the dog is supposed to be trying to tell Jules something: 'le chien [...] le regardait avidement comme s'il avait voulu lui parler' (I, p. 352). At first he combines powerful looks with barkings and howlings, but as this fails to elicit comprehension the emphasis is centred on the material qualities of his gaze, so that even when Jules thinks the dog has gone, the dog's eyes suddenly appear in the dark:

il s'en déversait une effusion sympathique qui se produisait de plus en plus, s'élargissant toujours et vous envahissant avec une séduction infinie [...]

Il n'y avait plus de cris, la bête était muette, et ne faisait plus rien que d'élargir cette pupille jaune dans laquelle il lui semblait qu'il se mirait; l'étonnement s'échangeait, ils se confrontaient tous deux, se demandant l'un à l'autre ce qu'on ne se dit pas. (p. 353)

What is thematized here ('une séduction infinie', 'l'étonnement s'échangeait'), as in so many of the preceding examples, is the ideal relationship between beholder and aesthetic object, elaborated metaphorically as a particular way of relating to people, objects and the natural world, all of which yield something in return: 'La sève des arbres vous entre au cœur par les longs regards stupides que l'on tient sur eux' (*Corr.* (B) II, p. 415 (1853)). But the most important yield is the reverie that Flaubert regarded as the supreme goal of art: 'J'admire cette manière à la fois véhémente et contenue, cette sympathie qui descend jusqu'aux êtres les plus infimes et donne une pensée aux paysages. On voit et on rêve' (*Corr. Suppl.* I, p. 318 (1863)). The reader's relationship with the literary work is invariably expressed through visual images, and 'le regard', closely related to the downgrading of an intellectual interpretation of the world, is central to Flaubert's aesthetic: 'Il fut un temps où j'aurais fait beaucoup plus de réflexions que je n'en fais maintenant [...] j'aurais peut-être plus réfléchi et moins regardé. Au contraire, j'ouvre les yeux sur tout, naïvement et simplement, ce qui est peut-être supérieur' (*Corr.* (B) I, p. 226 (1845)). Flaubert's seduction of the reader, accomplished with the aid of the physical qualities of his prose, is intended to induce a state of mute contemplation, and mindlessness, deliberate or otherwise, is clearly no disadvantage.

4

ENDLESS ILLUSIONS

Jean Ricardou tends to evaluate literature by its degree of self-representation: the major work is a book composed in such a way that it can support its own *dédoublement* and the inclusion of various fragments of itself; it is one that aspires to the seemingly impossible notion of a 'book within a book' (1967, p. 190). This normally takes the form of intense exploitation of the device now known as the *mise en abyme*: from play within a play, story within a story, or picture within a picture, the *mise en abyme* escalates in the *nouveau roman* into a profusion of explanatory metaphors and internal references. While I have tended so far to indicate ways in which the supposed modernity of Flaubert has been overplayed, in this chapter I shall consider the possibility that the ideal book about nothing, 'sans attache extérieure' (*Corr.* (B) II, p. 31 (1852)), might logically refer only to itself, and could usefully be viewed as an organized tautology. But just as I have already claimed that Flaubert's characters are accomplices of a certain sort of writing, here I shall explore another area of complicity. I shall seek to demonstrate that Flaubert's complicated networks of internal references, reflections and repetitions depend for their operation on the fictional behaviour and psychologies of his main protagonists.

An example from *Madame Bovary* illustrates precisely the overall effect of a novel which reflects and repeats itself, and the different mechanisms of repetition through which Flaubert typically organizes his representations. This is the description of the barrel-organ which occurs towards the end of the first part of the novel, at the period when Emma, as the ball at La Vaubyessard fades into the distance, becomes increasingly depressed:

Dans l'après-midi, quelquefois, une tête d'homme apparaissait derrière les vitres de la salle, tête hâlée, à favoris noirs, et qui souriait lentement d'un large sourire doux à dents blanches. Une valse aussitôt commençait, et, sur l'orgue, dans un petit salon, des danseurs hauts comme le doigt, femmes en turban rose, Tyroliens en jacquette, singes en habit noir, messieurs en culotte courte, tournaient, tournaient entre les fauteuils, les canapés, les consoles, se répétant dans les morceaux de miroir que raccordait à leurs angles un filet de papier doré. (I, p. 596)

Framed by the window through which it is watched (and into which it appears), this three-dimensional model and representation *en abyme* is clearly a replica of the ball at La Vaubyessard. More precisely it reproduces the high point of that occasion, the waltz with the Vicomte, the words used (themselves a repetition): 'tournaient, tournaient' picking up the 'Ils tournaient: tout tournait' of the original description of the waltz (p. 592). This particular syntactic pattern occurs elsewhere in the novel, for example the 'Ils allaient, ils allaient' of Emma's repeated night-time dream of eloping with Rodolphe (p. 640), the memory (inspired by her father's letter) of a repeated series of summer evenings when the foals 'galopaient, galopaient' (p. 632), and in the description of the endless whirring of Binet's lathe: 'les deux roues tournaient, ronflaient' (p. 677). The words are literally repeated when Emma has just left Rodolphe for the last time. Here she has an hallucinatory experience of being surrounded by balls of fire which 'tournaient, tournaient' with Rodolphe's face appearing in the middle of each and proliferating to infinity (p. 680). Perhaps the most important feature of the barrel organ description is the detail that the scene and all its implied repetitions are reflected to infinity in an arrangement of concentric mirrors: 'se répétant dans les morceaux de miroir que raccordait à leurs angles un filet de papier doré'. For these mirrorings of the waltz parody the infinite internal reflections which could be said to operate, within the text at large, through a structure of repetitions.[1] What is more, the man with the barrel organ does not appear behind the window on an isolated afternoon but 'quelquefois'. In other words the description in its entirety is already an iterative one, containing within itself its own repetition.

To sort out different kinds of repetition, it is helpful to use Genette's terminology from the discussion of 'frequency' in his 'Discours du récit' (1972, pp. 145–182). Frequency, order and duration are subsections of his first major category of verbal aspect: tense. This deals with the temporal relations between the discourse and the supposedly real events of the story, between the 'telling time' and the 'told time'. The repetition of events in a novel is related to two sorts of frequency: that of the event recounted and that of its recounting. In practice this seems reducible to two alternatives: an event can happen once in the story but be recounted a number of times ('repetitive narrative'), or it can happen a number of times in the actual story but only be

recounted once, or not so much 'une fois' as 'en une fo[
narrative'). Genette's own thesis in 'Discours du récit' is
abstract theory of time and memory serves a formal i[
organization of time in the novel as much as some deep [
truth. Now while both mechanisms of repetition (repetitiv
narrative) are important to all of Flaubert's mature works, where they
have been recognized they seem to have been given an exclusively
psychological interpretation. My own argument will be that the
functioning of repetition as a formal device does not exclude but tends
to subsume many thematic readings, and that Flaubert's characters,
through their particular psychological traits, are responsible for
making it work.

The commonest instance of repetitive narrative in Flaubert's works
is the sudden simultaneous influx of past memories:

Les premiers mois de son mariage, ses promenades à cheval dans la forêt,
le Vicomte qui valsait, et Lagardy chantant, tout repassa devant ses yeux.

(I, p. 670)

Carthage, Mégara, sa maison, sa chambre et les campagnes qu'elle avait
traversées tourbillonnaient dans sa mémoire en images tumultueuses et nettes
cependant.

(I, p. 760)

Mais, peu à peu, ses espérances et ses souvenirs, Nogent, la rue de Choiseul,
Mme Arnoux, sa mère, tout se confondait.

(II, p. 45)

Alors une faiblesse l'arrêta; et la misère de son enfance, la déception du
premier amour, le départ de son neveu, la mort de Virginie, comme les flots
d'une marée, revinrent à la fois, et, lui montant à la gorge, l'étouffaient.

(II, p. 175)

J. C. Lapp has accurately described the effect of these passages, yet
he interprets them, in *Madame Bovary*, as a sign of Emma's futile
struggle against the 'sickness of the memory', ending in a 'final
triumph of past over present' (1956, p. 326). For Poulet these memory
sequences are instances of Flaubert's portrayal of 'time', of his ability
to create 'une densité spatiale et temporelle si particulière', and 'la
profondeur de la durée' (1950, pp. 312 and 316).[2]

But in these passages it is not only the character who relives his
past, for the novel uses these *reprises* to motivate the retracing of
its own steps. The arbitrary repeated descriptions of a *nouveau roman*
like Robbe-Grillet's *La Jalousie* (where any attempt to explain these
solely by the notion of a deranged reflecting consciousness would
surely be a misreading), are not conceivable in a nineteenth-century
novel. Nevertheless I would maintain that the aesthetic effect of

Flaubert's *reprises* is not so different. Repetition is a basic means of organization of any art-form (most obviously of music), and is certainly a common way of creating pleasure (for example in poetry). The *laisses similaires* of the *Chanson de Roland* are a famous example of acute aesthetic effect achieved by repetition, but accentuated by minute variations. When Emma goes to the opera in *Madame Bovary*, despite the pleasure of watching and listening to Lucie, she gains her acutest enjoyment from the chorus: 'les voix des femmes, répétant ses paroles, reprenaient en chœur, délicieusement' (I, p. 651). Similarly, when Flaubert himself describes a sort of shadow theatre seen in Carthage, the enjoyment provided by the main character is quite surpassed by the chorus: 'Ce qu'il y avait de beau, c'étaient les trois musiciens qui, de temps à autre et à intervalles réguliers, reprenaient ce qu'il disait, ou mieux réfléchissaient tout haut à la façon du chœur; cela était très dramatique et il me sembla que j'avais compris' (II, p. 710). Thus characters who supposedly suffer from a pathological sickness of the memory, contribute to the pleasurable effects of Flaubert's writing and, by providing him with elliptical summaries of events, collaborate in the organization of the plot. When the smell of Rodolphe's hair-dressing sets off Emma's reverie at the *Comices agricoles*, she fuses memories of the Vicomte and Léon with the presence of Rodolphe; by noticing the *Hirondelle* in the distance she refers forward to the story to come, and in her generally confused and hallucinated state motivates a fine passage dense with echoes from the rest of the novel:

Elle distinguait dans ses yeux des petits rayons d'or, s'irradiant tout entour de ses pupilles noires, et même elle sentait le parfum de la pommade qui lustrait sa chevelure. Alors une mollesse la saisit, elle se rappela ce vicomte qui l'avait fait valser à la Vaubyessard, et dont la barbe exhalait, comme ces cheveux-là, cette odeur de vanille et de citron; et, machinalement, elle entreferma les paupières pour le mieux respirer. Mais, dans ce geste qu'elle fit en se cabrant sur sa chaise, elle aperçut au loin, tout au fond de l'horizon, la vieille diligence l'*Hirondelle*, qui descendait lentement la côte des Leux, en traînant après soi un long panache de poussière. C'était dans cette voiture jaune que Léon, si souvent, était revenu vers elle; et par cette route là-bas qu'il était parti pour toujours! Elle crut le voir en face, à sa fenêtre, puis tout se confondit, des nuages passèrent; il lui sembla qu'elle tournait encore dans la valse, sous le feu des lustres, au bras du vicomte, et que Léon n'était pas loin, qu'il allait venir... et cependant elle sentait toujours la tête de Rodolphe à côté d'elle. La douceur de cette sensation pénétrait ainsi ses désirs d'autrefois, et comme des grains de sable sous un coup de vent, ils tourbillonnaient dans la bouffée subtile du parfum qui se répandait sur son âme. (I, p. 624)

Homais's newspaper articles on the *Comices agrico*͵
the club foot operation (p. 634) provide ironic written
these important episodes. Indeed a reference in Flauberᵗ
dence to the former underlines his functional conception
'Je ne suis pas mécontent de mon article de Homais (inᵈ
citations). Il rehausse les comices et les fait paraître plus ͼ
qu'il les résume' (*Corr.* (B) II, p. 473 (1853)). Emma's last ͼˢ involve
a similar sort of repetition:

d'abord sur les yeux, qui avaient tant convoité toutes les somptuosités ter-
restres; plus sur les narines, friandes de brises tièdes et de senteurs amoureuses;
puis sur la bouche, qui s'était ouverte pour le mensonge, qui avait gémi
d'orgueil et crié dans la luxure; puis sur les mains, qui se délectaient aux
contacts suaves, et enfin sur la plante des pieds, si rapides autrefois quand
elle courait à l'assouvissement de ses désirs, et qui maintenant ne marcheraient
plus.   (I, p. 684)

Consider too Rodolphe's overview of the probable history of Emma's
marriage, the likely course of his seduction of Emma, and the inevitable
problems that would subsequently arise ('les encombrements du
plaisir, entrevus en perspective'):

— Je le crois très bête [Charles]. Elle en est fatiguée sans doute. Il porte
des ongles sales et une barbe de trois jours. Tandis qu'il trottine à ses malades,
elle reste à ravauder des chaussettes. Et on s'ennuie! On voudrait habiter la
ville, danser la polka tous les soirs! Pauvre petite femme! Ça baille après
l'amour, comme une carpe après l'eau sur une table de cuisine. Avec trois
mots de galanterie, cela vous adorerait, j'en suis sûr! ce serait tendre!
charmant!... Oui, mais comment s'en débarrasser ensuite?   (I, p. 618)

Here Rodolphe's 'intelligence perspicace' effectively sums up Emma's
story in a few cynical lines.

The financial ruins described in *Madame Bovary* and *L'Éducation
sentimentale,* and the death of Mme Aubain in *Un Cœur simple,*
provide the necessary excuse for inventories of furniture, ornaments
and personal effects which have played an important part in the story:

Ils commencèrent par le cabinet de Bovary et n'inscrivirent point la tête
phrénologique, qui fut considérée comme *instrument de sa profession*; mais
ils comptèrent dans la cuisine les plats, les marmites, les chaises, les flambeaux,
et, dans sa chambre à coucher, toutes les babioles de l'étagère. Ils examinèrent
ses robes, le linge, le cabinet de toilette; et son existence, jusque dans ses
recoins les plus intimes, fut, comme un cadavre que l'on autopsie, étalée tout
au long aux regards de ces trois hommes.   (I, p. 674)

Le fauteuil de Madame, son guéridon, sa chaufferette, les huit chaises, étaient
partis! La place des gravures se dessinait en carrés jaunes au milieu des

oisons. Ils avaient emporté les deux couchettes, avec leurs matelas, et dans le placard on ne voyait plus rien de toutes les affaires de Virginie! Félicité remonta les étages, ivre de tristesse.   (II, p. 176)

For Victor Brombert, the auction sale of Mme Arnoux's belongings symbolizes the 'impression of a whole life being liquidated' (1966, p. 149). But most obviously these literal inventories and 'autopsies' (always situated near the end of the works in which they occur), emerge as inventories of the works themselves.

Frédéric's own perception of the auction sale reveals the fetishistic nature of his obsession with Mme Arnoux:

Quand Frédéric entra, les jupons, les fichus, les mouchoirs et jusqu'aux chemises étaient passés de main en main, retournés; quelquefois, on les jetait de loin, et des blancheurs traversaient l'air tout à coup. Ensuite on vendit ses robes, puis un de ses chapeaux dont la plume cassée retombait, puis ses fourrures, puis trois paires de bottines; − et le partage de ces reliques, où il trouvait confusément les formes de ses membres, lui semblait une atrocité, comme s'il avait vu des corbeaux déchiquetant son cadavre [...] Ainsi disparurent les uns après les autres, le grand tapis bleu semé de camélias, que ses pieds mignons frôlaient en venant vers lui, la petite bergère de tapisserie où il s'asseyait en face d'elle quand ils étaient seuls; les deux écrans de la cheminée, dont l'voire étaient rendu plus doux par le contact de ses mains; une pelotte de velours, encore hérissée d'épingles.   (II, p. 158)

His attachment to Mme Arnoux's clothing, and to the furniture and ornaments that he would notice when he visited her, is recalled and developed here. Indeed Flaubert invariably emphasizes his characters' concern for traces that the loved person has either actually left or is imagined to have left on objects they have touched and in rooms they have inhabited. This is a theme which the two versions of *L'Éducation* very obviously share (Henry and Mme Renaud prefiguring Frédéric and Mme Arnoux):

'Ma chambre, depuis ce moment, est pleine de ce bonheur, je retrouve dans l'air quelque chose d'elle. Si je m'assieds sur un meuble, mes membres se posent aux places où elle a posé les siens; le jour, je marche sur les pavés où elle a marché et la nuit je m'étale avec joie sur ce lit, dont les draps sont tièdes encore, sur cet oreiller qu'elle a parfumé avec ses cheveux. J'avais déchiré sa collerette, elle l'ôta et m'en fit cadeau, je l'ai, je la garderai'.
                                                                    (I, p. 312)[3]

Quand il fut remonté dans son cabinet, il contempla le fauteuil où elle s'était assise et tous les objets qu'elle avait touchés. Quelque chose d'elle circulait autour de lui. La caresse de sa présence durait encore.   (II, p. 76)

Such passages repeat characters in their absence and rec; descriptions. This is surely the function of the vast network nal references in the 1869 *Éducation*: the identical furnis Rosanette's and Mme Arnoux's homes and the movement of ε laden objects like the chandelier and especially the silver 'cι ___. . Evidently it is the fetishistic bent of Frédéric's mind and manner of loving that, along with his inability to choose between the different women, motivates and supports the poetic atmosphere of the novel that is so tied up with the description of interior settings.

It is Charles's morbidly fetishistic behaviour after Emma's death that fills the final pages of *Madame Bovary* with echoes and reminders of Emma:

Félicité portait maintenant les robes de Madame; non pas toutes, car il en avait gardé quelques-unes, et il les allait voir dans son cabinet de toilette, où il s'enfermait; elle était à peu près de sa taille, souvent Charles, en l'apercevant par derrière, était saisi d'une illusion et répétait:

— Oh! reste! reste! (I, p. 689)

Pour lui plaire, comme si elle vivait encore, il adopta ses prédilections, ses idées, il s'acheta des bottes vernies, il prit l'usage des cravates blanches. Il mettait du cosmétique à ses moustaches, il souscrivit comme elle des billets à ordre. Elle le corrompait par delà le tombeau. (I, p. 690)[5]

When his memory of Emma begins to fade, still he dreams about her every night, and each night it is inevitably the same dream. Indeed Charles is an exemplary repeater from his first entry into the novel. It is because he is 'stupid' and inarticulate that he is given the suitable punishment of *copying* out twenty times the verb 'ridiculus sum' (p. 575) (the written repetition which becomes an aesthetic principle by the time of *Bouvard et Pécuchet*). Returning from seeing Emma at Les Bertaux, he 'reprit une à une les phrases qu'elle avait dites', finds he cannot understand them, so just repeats them over and over (p. 582). He always imagines her just as he first saw her, and after their marriage, when he returns home in the evenings, he recounts one after another all the people he has met, the villages he has visited, and the prescriptions he has written. Further 'ses expansions étaient devenues régulières; il l'embrassait à de certaines heures' (p. 589). Unlike Emma and Homais, who already choose names for their children after various models, Charles wants the baby named after Emma — clearly he wishes her to be an exact replica, as proved by his own reiterated night-time fantasy in which he imagines them side by side like two identical sisters.

The description of Félicité's room, in *Un Cœur simple*, as a chapel

61

or bazaar full of religious objects and 'choses hétéroclites' (II, p. 175), is doubtless the most developed example in Flaubert's works of an inventory-like description gathering together and repeating every element that has been important in the story: a shell box given by Victor, the picture-book geography, Virginie's plush hat which Félicité chooses to hang in front of a mirror which would reflect all this, and finally the object on which all the fetishistic themes of the story converge, the stuffed parrot:

> On voyait contre les murs: des chapelets, des médailles, plusieurs bonnes Vierges, un bénitier de noix de coco; sur la commode, couverte d'un drap comme un autel, la boîte en coquillages que lui avait donnée Victor; puis un arrosoir et un ballon, des cahiers d'écriture, la géographie en estampes, une paire de bottines; et au clou du miroir, accroché par ses rubans, le petit chapeau de peluche! Félicité poussait même ce genre de respect si loin, qu'elle conservait une des redingotes de Monsieur. Toutes les vieilleries dont ne voulait plus Mme Aubain, elle les prenait pour sa chambre. C'est ainsi qu'il y avait des fleurs artificielles au bord de la commode, et le portrait du comte d'Artois dans l'enfoncement de la lucarne.
>
> Au moyen d'une planchette, Loulou fut établi sur un corps de cheminée qui avançait dans l'appartement. Chaque matin, en s'éveillant, elle l'apercevait à la clarté de l'aube, et se rappelait alors les jours disparus, et d'insignifiantes actions jusqu'en leurs moindres détails, sans douleur, pleine de tranquillité.
>
> (II, pp. 175–6)

If we accept the positive role of a passage like this in the overall organization of the story (a dense network of minute connecting details and metonymic processes), are we not invited to give a positive evaluation both of the theme of fetishism which runs through the story, and of its most exemplary exponent: Félicité herself?[6] The cult of material souvenirs runs from the opening description of Mme Aubain's house, where the 'souvenir de "Monsieur"' at first overawes Félicité (p. 167), through Félicité's own escalating fetishism (the lock of Virginie's hair, Virginie's hat), through the repeated references to the *Fête-Dieu* and the final overladen *reposoir* reminiscent of Félicité's room (the pyramid shape, the nature of the offerings, Loulou as the ultimate relic), the description of which precedes and produces Félicité's final vision of the gigantic parrot. Félicité's room is her own original and idiosyncratic creation, and she is personally responsible for the two important representations of Loulou: first, in having him stuffed as a splendid replica of his former self, and finally in fostering his framing as an actual picture. From her initial association of Loulou with the *image d'Épinal* of the Holy Ghost ('sa ressemblance lui parut encore plus manifeste sur une image d'Épinal, représentant le baptême de Notre-Seigneur. Avec ses ailes de pourpre et son corps d'émeraude, c'était vraiment le portrait de Loulou' (p. 176)), she goes on to buy the picture and to hang it in place of the portrait of the Comte d'Artois, next to the parrot himself. Since she is then able to embrace them both with one look, this confusion between them leads to a displaced framing of Loulou. If the final identification of the parrot and the Holy Ghost in the closing apotheosis − typically and ironically intensified as an extraordinary illusion by the choice of the adjective 'gigantesque' (p. 177) − is totally appropriate, this is because it is an *aesthetic* identification prepared for by the careful composition of the story.[7]

It is obvious that Félicité's story is a repeated cycle of loves, deaths, and displacements of affection.[8] The fact that Paul one day blows cigar smoke in Loulou's face is a good example of the minute network of references: Victor, Havana ('À cause des cigares, elle imaginait La Havane un pays où l'on ne fait pas autre chose que de fumer' (p. 171)), America, the prefect who had been consul in America, Loulou himself. While the name Virginie is ironically connected with Bernardin de Saint-Pierre's *Paul et Virginie*, another obvious association is with Félicité herself: it is stressed that she remains a virgin in her romance with Théodore, the description of Virginie's First Communion − during which Félicité achieves a complete identification with Virginie − uses the word ('le troupeau des vierges' (p. 170)), and Félicité at one stage wants to join 'les demoiselles de la Vierge' (p. 176). The important *mise en abyme* of the stained glass window in the church, in which 'le Saint-Esprit dominait la Vierge' (p. 169),[9] clearly relates to the 'transcendental' meaning of the story established by the ironic ending: 'elle crut voir, dans les cieux entr'ouverts, un perroquet gigantesque, planant au-dessus de sa tête' (p. 177).

But the essential point is that the story's formal mechanism of repetition and transference takes place with Félicité's aid, for it is motivated by her typical mental behaviour. Flaubert describes her in a scenario as having: 'Manière de penser comme en rêve. Les idées les plus disparates se succèdent' (B.N. n.a.fr. 23663, fol. 381ᵛ). It is the combination of her tendency to distraction (going back to shut the unlocked door, though rushing to Virginie's death bed), with her fetishistic attachments (since fetishism is already metonymy), that keeps up the process of substitution. It is the discovery of Virginie's plush hat, and Félicité's request to keep it, that allows the transfer of affection to Mme Aubain, and the tears that she sheds on her mistress's death ('Félicité la pleura, comme on ne pleure pas les maîtres' (p. 176)), act as a displacement of her suppressed grief for Victor and Virginie. When she is convinced that because Victor and Virginie are linked in her heart their destiny must be the same, this prophesies and seems almost to control events: when Victor dies, Virginie's death follows straight on. When Félicité is 'stupidly' worried that Victor will never return from such a long voyage she is right: he does not return. When Félicité is waiting for news of the dying Virginie she has an almost clichéd 'literary' idea: 'Puis elle resta dans l'auberge, croyant que des inconnus apporteraient une lettre' (p. 172). This does not happen here, but her clichéd notion is later incorporated into the narrative: 'Une nuit, le conducteur de la malle-poste annonça dans Pont l'Évêque la Révolution de Juillet' (p. 173). The metonymic process happens automatically in Mme Aubain's dream after Virginie's death, in which her long-dead husband is transposed into the recently deceased Victor (he is dressed as a sailor). Mme Aubain needs these dreams to make connections, but Félicité already thinks in this way and is constantly creating instinctive associations and repetitions. The final merging of the parrot and the Holy Ghost, the climax of the metonymic processes of Flaubert's story, is something Félicité has been working on all along.

Félicité's role is therefore an aesthetic one, for she is largely responsible for the self-representation of the story. She is very much caught up in repetition, functioning almost automatically in her regular habits and unchanging daily routine, getting on with her usual work when Victor dies (repeating 'Pauvre petit gars! pauvre petit gars!' (p. 172)), saying the same prayers over and over throughout two nights when Virginie dies. She learns the catechism 'parrot fashion' by hearing it repeated (at one remove since she listens to the children learning it in this way). The repetitions of language itself are parodied in Loulou, and whereas we are told that parrots are supposed to be called Jacquot, it is no surprise that this one is called Loulou, a name based on repetition. Félicité teaches him to repeat a set of three phrases (learned, of course, by hearing them repeated), which are not as meaningless as they might at first seem, since they sum up and repeat the important aspects of Félicité's story: 'Charmant garçon! Serviteur, monsieur! Je vous salue, Marie!' (p. 174). Loulou and Félicité have conversations based on the endless repetition of three phrases, and just as Loulou's laughter at the sight of Bourais echoes round the village, so these phrases echo round the story. When Félicité goes deaf the parrot entertains her by imitating voices and sounds themselves containing repeated sounds, such as the 'tic tac du tournebroche' and Mme Aubain shouting 'la porte! la porte!' to Félicité (p. 175).[10]

Thus Félicité and Loulou are between them given the task of operating the story's internal reflections. It is Félicité's inarticulacy, her inability to cope with the concept of symbolism (the map of the world, the Holy Ghost as fire, breath or bird), and the fetishistic tendency of her mind, which combine to give her a central aesthetic function in Flaubert's story.

I shall turn more briefly to the other sort of repetition, iterative narrative which (by use of the frequentative imperfect tense), repeats 'en une fois' what happens many times over. Discussing its overwhelming importance for Proust, Genette identifies Flaubert as the precursor:

> Comme la description, le récit itératif est, dans le roman traditionnel, *au service* du récit 'proprement dit', qui est le récit singulatif. Le premier romancier qui ait entrepris de l'émanciper de cette dépendance fonctionnelle est évidemment Flaubert dans *Madame Bovary*, où des pages comme celles qui raconte la vie d'Emma au couvent, à Tostes avant et après le bal à la Vaubyessard, ou ses jeudis à Rouen avec Léon, prennent une amplitude et une autonomie tout à fait inusitées.   (1972, p. 148)

But a problem arises over its evaluation. Roger Huss, analysing the 'Thursdays at Rouen' chapter which describes only once and in very specific detail what is supposed to happen every Thursday, picks up details such as extracts of direct conversation, sudden movements of emotion, and the wet roofs in the view of Rouen, none of which could be literally present every Thursday.[11] He concludes, however, 'that Flaubert's use of the iterative imperfect to convey highly particularized events is consistent with a sense of *déjà vu* and tedium, with an inability to believe in the originality of any event' (1977, p. 146). Tony Tanner's extremely negative evaluation of the function of repetition in *Madame Bovary* shares this general view that repetition is at the service of a world-view whereby 'nothing ever changes'. Emma's life is deemed a 'vicious downward spiral of devaluation through repetition' (1979, p. 376), Binet is 'the incarnation of the ultimate deadly drive to duplicate' (p. 257), and since 'copying devalues by repetition; continual identity of repetition ends in the annihilation of meaning' (p. 246). Charles as a character prepares the reader 'for a novel concerning a mode of life that in a profound sense is without novelty' (pp. 251–2); 'fetishism, repetition and insentience take the place of authentic interhuman contact' (p. 271), and 'what is briefly suggested here is that what supersedes the demise or collapse or evacuation of imagination is – continual repetition' (pp. 274–5).[12]

This barrage of quotations from Tanner illustrates an extreme version of the view that I wish to refute in this chapter. Fictional characters who are caught up in repetition invite a more sympathetic reading, if the role of repetition in Flaubert's aesthetic is in fact a positive one. Bruce F. Kawin, in his book on repetition in film and literature, distinguishes between 'repetitious': 'when a word, percept, or experience is repeated with less impact at each recurrence; repeated to no particular end, out of a failure of invention or sloppiness of thought', and 'repetitive': 'when a word, percept, or experience is repeated with equal or greater force at each occurence' (1972, p. 4). This division of the semantic field may be confusing, in that it does not correspond to ordinary usage of the two words. However, Kawin's distinction between two sorts of repetition – one negative and one positive – offers a useful approach to the evaluation of repetition in Flaubert's works.

The problem is that in *Madame Bovary* at least the 'repetitious' *is* an important part of Emma's experience of life, and boredom and monotony *are* powerfully conveyed by the iterative imperfect. If one wanted to argue that this was its main use, Emma's walks with her greyhound during her first miserable period at Tostes would be an excellent example (I, p. 589). The fact that these walks are repeated multiplies the depressing set of repetitions they already contain. Each time Emma begins by looking around in the hope that something has changed, but nothing ever has. Each time she repeats to herself 'Pourquoi, mon Dieu, me suis-je mariée?', and recalls her life at school (a *reprise* of the chapter recalling her early life), a passage itself ending with a repeated 'Comme c'était loin, tout cela! comme c'était loin!'. The bored yawns of her greyhound cause her to liken him to herself, and he operates as her double, his circles in the country specifically complementing those of her depressed reverie.

But the iterative imperfect could be considered at the service of the theme of monotony only if it were used solely in this connection, which is not at all the case. That repetition serves boredom in *Madame Bovary*, obsession in *La Légende de Saint Julien l'Hospitalier* (see below), and ecstasy in the Auteuil episode in *L'Éducation sentimentale* (see chapter 5), already suggests that repetition should be extracted as the common denominator, and assessed accordingly. But even in *Madame Bovary* repetition just as frequently coincides with moments of intense pleasure and satisfaction (the repetitions of the ball, for instance, never devalue it). The iteration of the Thursdays at Rouen can hardly be seen as an attack on the non-originality of events, for it is the high point of Emma's affair with Léon, as is illustrated by the agony of her weekly return to Yonville. Indeed the description of the view of Rouen, which is so specific in its meteorological details, coincides with one of the rare moments for Emma of joyful, pantheistic expansion of the self:

Quelque chose de vertigineux se dégageait pour elle de ces existences amassées, et son cœur s'en gonflait abondamment, comme si les cent milles âmes qui palpitaient là eussent envoyé toutes à la fois la vapeur des passions qu'elle leur supposait. Son amour s'agrandissait devant l'espace, et s'emplissait de tumulte aux bourdonnements vagues qui montaient. Elle le renversait au dehors, sur les places, sur les promenades, sur les rues, et la vieille cité normande s'étalait à ses yeux comme une capitale démesurée, comme une Babylone où elle entrait.   (I, p. 663)

Similarly, the evenings spent with Rodolphe by the river provide a striking example of a lyrical use of the iterative imperfect, the effect of which is multiplied, *en abyme*, by the further degrees of iteration contained inside the description, by subdivisions marked by adverbs of frequency such as 'parfois' and 'de temps à autre':

Les étoiles brillaient à travers les branches de jasmin sans feuilles. Ils entendaient derrière eux la rivière qui coulait, et, de temps à autre, sur la berge, le claquement des roseaux secs. Des massifs d'ombre, çà et là, se bombaient dans l'obscurité, et parfois, frissonnant tous d'un seul mouvement, ils se dressaient et se penchaient comme d'immenses vagues noires qui se fussent avancées pour les recouvrir. Le froid de la nuit les faisait s'étendre davantage; les soupirs de leurs lèvres leur semblaient plus forts; leurs yeux, qu'ils entrevoyaient à peine, leur paraissaient plus grands, et, au milieu du silence, il y avait des paroles dites tout bas qui tombaient sur leur âme avec une sonorité cristalline et qui s'y répercutaient en vibrations multipliées.   (p. 631)

'Vibrations multipliées' sums up the effect of these passages. When Léon leaves Yonville, Emma is plunged into 'cette douleur, enfin, que vous apportent l'interruption de tout mouvement accoutumé, la cessation brusque d'une vibration prolongée' (p. 616). Reverberation is suggested by the little phrase that often appears almost as a tic of style: 'çà et là', itself containing a repeated sound.[13] The account of Emma's 'honeymoon' with Léon again describes once what actually happens three days running, and the profusion of tiny regularly repeated sounds which stand out against the evening silence ('comme un battement de métronome', 'son petit clapotement doux' etc. (p. 661)), have already been referred to in chapter 3. When this iterative description is made to contain one specific occasion on which the moon appeared ('Une fois, la lune parut'), this, in its turn, contains a sentence beginning 'parfois', in which Emma constantly disappears and reappears in alternating shadow and moonlight. Within the general framework of the use of the iterative imperfect, which by a simple morphological addition to the verb can create multiple, simultaneous repetitions of events, subdivision into new sorts of repetition seems to be a potentially infinite process.

Finally, a repeated reading of the whole work would be the last level on which all of the contained representations are multiplied, be they the simultaneous representations of iterative narrative, or the consecutive recalls of repetitive narrative.[14] Indeed, it seems reasonable to assume that the author of such carefully and lengthily written works – the Flaubert whose adherence to *l'art pour l'art* was largely to a non-commercial sort of literature – would ideally wish his novels to be read *over and over again*.[15]

Flaubert's use of language, with its characteristic repetition of certain stylistic effects,[16] has its own role to play, as we saw earlier, in seducing the reader into the hypnotic state in which he will correctly apprehend this plethora of represented repetitions. It may seem, however, that by limiting the foregoing discussion to the role of repetition in the representation of the illusion of reality, I have avoided the implications of the written repetition or copying on which *Bouvard et Pécuchet* is founded, for instance the indiscriminate copying of random written material that was to form the second volume. This could be seen as undermining the very notion of representation, as being nearer to 'anti' than 'self' representation.[17] Yet there is more going on in *Bouvard et Pécuchet* than straightforward rewriting, and the existing volume of the novel still has an important story, however full of copies and repetitions. Even the examples of the pre-eminence of the signifier, discussed in chapter 3, are largely thematic, for example Bouvard and Pécuchet's pleasure in playing with the echo which they accidentally create during the landscaping of their garden. When, on their first night in the garden, two shadows on the wall both enlarge and repeat Bouvard and Pécuchet's movements – 'Quelquefois, une araignée fuyait tout à coup sur le mur, et les deux ombres de leurs corps s'y dessinaient agrandies, en répétant leurs gestes' (II, p. 207) – this is simply an excellent example of *mise en abyme*. Although Flaubert may hover in this text on the brink of a radically modern conception,[18] *Bouvard et Pécuchet* is nevertheless largely a traditional representation, albeit one which ironizes and foregrounds the artificiality of its representations.

For if Bouvard and Pécuchet are established as ironic artist figures, they are caught up in producing illusions and representations as well as in pure wallowing in the physical qualities of language. Consider

their special act for privileged visitors to their museum (which creates
the desired 'ébahissement'):

> Bouvard s'éloigna et reparut affublé d'une couverture de laine, puis s'agenouilla
> devant le prie-Dieu, les coudes en dehors, la face dans les mains, la lueur du
> soleil tombant sur sa calvitie; et il avait conscience et cet effet, car il dit:
> — Est-ce que je n'ai pas l'air d'une moine du moyen âge?
> Ensuite il leva le front obliquement, les yeux noyés, faisant prendre à sa
> figure une expression mystique. On entendit dans le corridor la voix grave
> de Pécuchet:
> — N'aie pas peur, c'est moi.
> Et il entra, la tête couverte d'un casque: un pot de fer à oreillons pointus.
> Bouvard ne quitta pas le prie-Dieu. Les deux autres restaient debout. Une
> minute passa dans l'ébahissement. (p. 235)

All of their works of art are in the best Flaubertian tradition, but
especially those from the period of landscape gardening. One is even
constructed in the manner of Flaubert's ideal masterpiece as pyramid,
laboriously constructed:

> Ils avaient été sur les rives de l'Orne choisir des granits, les avaient cassés,
> numerotés, rapportés eux-mêmes dans une charrette, puis avaient joint les
> morceaux avec du ciment, en les accumulant les uns par-dessus les autres,
> et au milieu du gazon se dressait un rocher, pareil à une gigantesque pomme
> de terre. (p. 215)[19]

Nor should Ricardou disapprove of their foregrounding of artificiality:

> Les deux premiers ifs de la grande allée, qui, la veille encore, étaient
> sphériques, avaient la forme des paons, et un cornet avec deux boutons de
> porcelaine figuraient le bec et les yeux. (p. 216)

> Le rocher, comme une montagne, occupait le gazon, le tombeau faisait un
> cube au milieu des épinards, le pont vénitien un accent circonflexe par-dessus
> les haricots, et la cabane, au delà, une grande tache noire, car ils avaient
> incendié son toit de paille pour la rendre plus poétique [...] La pagode chinoise,
> peinte en rouge, semblait un phare sur le vigneau. (p. 217)

Bearing in mind the origins of the pagoda — 'Au sommet du vigneau,
six arbres équarris supportaient un chapeau de fer-blanc à pointes
retroussées, et le tout signifiait une pagode chinoise' (p. 215) — it can
be seen that this is an example of imitation at several removes, the
whole thing having been originally constructed with the aid of
Boitard's *L'Architecte des jardins*. It is also deliberately framed by
Bouvard and Pécuchet, who unveil it for the visitors: 'Pécuchet fit
un signe, les rideaux s'ouvrirent et le jardin apparut' (p. 217), while
the total effect coincides with Flaubert's often mentioned aesthetic
ideal: 'quelque chose d'effrayant'.

While all these examples are self-conscious parodies, their function is not different in kind from the many semi-ironic representations which fill the pages of *L'Éducation sentimentale* (Rosanette's portrait), or *Madame Bovary* (the wedding cake, the framed daguerrotype portrait of Charles, Emma's tomb, Homais's floral 'croix d'honneur', etc.). These more classical novels of representation support uses of *mise en abyme* which are the more radical for their apparently realist setting. Consider Charles's written instructions for Emma's burial in a nest of three coffins, or the 'hearts of women' passage in *L'Éducation sentimentale*, the unusual rhetoric of both providing fine formal set-pieces — images for a 'layering' of representations built into a 'book about nothing':

'Je veux qu'on l'enterre dans sa robe de noces, avec des souliers blancs, une couronne. On lui étalera ses cheveux sur ses épaules; trois cercueils, un de chêne, un d'acajou, un de plomb. Qu'on ne me dise rien, j'aurai de la force. On lui mettra par-dessus toute une grande pièce de velours vert. Je le veux. Faites-le.' (I, p. 685)

Les cœurs de femmes sont comme ces petits meubles à secret, pleins de tiroirs emboîtés les uns dans les autres; on se donne du mal, on se casse les ongles, et on trouve au fond quelque fleur désséchée, des brins de poussière – ou le vide! (II, p. 149)

But the most sustained experiment with *mise en abyme* occurs in *La Légende de Saint Julien l'Hospitalier*, which approximates to Ricardou's ideal of the work of art that can sustain its own radical *dédoublement*. Working alongside the title, which reveals that the story will chart Julien's accession to sainthood, are the three predictions which precede and control the working out of the story. For Ricardou the oracle (and *Oedipus Rex* is his main example), by containing the story in concentrated form, is a basic instance of *mise en abyme* (1967, pp. 176–9). The opening predictions are indeed fragmented throughout the story, before being gathered in again to other concentrated images. For example the prediction to Julien's mother: 'Réjouis-toi, ô mère! ton fils sera un saint!' (II, p. 178) is dispersed along a chain of religious references. The household is as well regulated as a monastery by Julien's mother, who often passes her time embroidering altar cloths. Over her bed hangs a religious relic (a martyr's bone) in a carbuncle frame, and over Julien's cradle hangs a dove-shaped lamp. The baby Julien resembles a little Jesus, and passing pilgrims tell tales of the Holy Manger and the Sepulchre. Julien's hunting manual with its question and answer format suggests a catechism manual, he commits his first sadistic murders at mass, and is actually praying when he hears the fox yelping and the ambiguous footsteps that tempt him out on the second fatal hunting expedition.[20] A cock crows just before the murder, an ivory Christ hangs in the death chamber (splattered with the parents' blood), and Julien leaves his written instructions for the funeral on a *prie-Dieu*. When he sets off over the river to fetch the leper the stormy weather, as in the biblical miracle, goes suddenly calm, the leper has a regal bearing and is covered in a sort of shroud, he eats bread, turns Julien's water into wine, and is finally transformed into Jesus Christ.

The father's prediction: 'Ah! ah! ton fils! ... beaucoup de sang! ... beaucoup de gloire! ... toujours heureux! la famille d'un empereur' (p. 178), ironically referred to as 'ces mots sans suite', contains the essential prophecy of much blood which, disguised by its association with the promise of glory and power, is in fact the blood which Julien will spill in the course of the story. This *mise en abyme* is fragmented into a widespread network of images of blood, redness, fire, sparks and light:[21] 'Dans l'illumination des flambeaux'; 'les prunelles flamboyantes' (p. 178); 'le ciel était rouge comme une nappe de sang' (p. 181); 'Il traversa des régions si torrides que sous l'ardeur du soleil des chevelures s'allumaient d'elles-mêmes, comme des flambeaux' (p. 182); 'Le soleil, tous les soirs, étalait du sang dans les nuages' (p. 186). The 'prunelles flamboyantes' of the beggar who speaks the prediction are passed to other key figures of the series: the father stag ('et, les yeux flamboyants' (p. 181)), the corpse of Julien's father ('une prunelle éteinte qui le brûla comme du feu' (p. 185)), and finally to the leper ('les deux yeux plus rouges que des charbons'; 'et ses yeux tout à coup prirent une clarté d'étoiles' (p. 186)). The blood references are gathered into a further *mise en abyme* in the death chamber: 'Le reflet écarlate du vitrail, alors frappé par le soleil, éclairait ces taches rouges, et en jetait de plus nombreuses dans tout l'appartement' (p. 185). The 'vitrail', a *mise en abyme* in itself (not only contained by and relating to the final stained glass window, but also, by its various open and shut positions, playing a causal role in the murder),[22] sheds a scarlet reflection which in turn lights up and multiplies the red stains throughout the room.

The connection between the hunting lust and the desire to kill the parents is underlined by the fact that Julien's father is 'toujours enveloppé d'une pelisse de renard' (p. 178) and that, as mentioned, it is a fox which tempts Julien back into hunting. The first description of the mother speaks of 'les *cornes* de son hennin' and 'la *queue* de sa robe' (p. 178, my emphases), and it is Julien's mistaking his mother for a stork (note the mother's 'bonnet à longues barbes' (p. 182)), which causes him to hurl his javelin at her (for despite his resolve not to kill any more animals, he had intended to kill this 'stork'). The family of deer which Julien kills are themselves a miniature replica of Julien's family (mother, father and child); and Shoshana Felman points out the link between the 'faon tacheté' and the 'signes particuliers' on Julien's skin (passed later via the leper to the table, dish and knife handle at the 'last supper') (1981, p.45). The murder of the deer foreshadows the main murder, so that in a sense the murder is already accomplished even as it is prophesied. This is typical of the way in which Ricardou suggests that the *mise en abyme* is the 'structural revolt' of a fragment which can unbalance the whole (1967, p.181).

The father stag's prediction, repeated three times to the accompaniment of a striking bell, is itself a set-piece of formal repetition: 'Maudit! maudit! maudit! Un jour, cœur féroce, tu assassineras ton père et ta mère' (p.181). This scene is exactly repeated at the end, when the leper calls three times to Julien in a voice with the intonation of a church bell. Julien is obsessed with the stag's prediction (as were the parents with theirs, simultaneously remembering them on the night of the murder). For Julien, after his marriage, this obsession produces a dream of killing animals, with an endless replay of the actual massacre inside each dream. After the parents' murder a dream endlessly repeats the actual event: 'Le soleil, tous les soirs, était du sang dans les nuages; et chaque nuit, en rêve, son parricide recommençait' (p.186). When Julien recalls his youth he sees himself, by an effect of *dédoublement*, as he was at the beginning of the story, standing between his parents and framed in a vine arbour. Each time this becomes a hallucination of the two corpses, on the appearance of which Julien repeats the lament: 'Ah, pauvre père, pauvre mère! pauvre mère!' (p.186).

A final pattern of images again suggests a formal mechanism of the story, culminating in the final face to face apotheosis of Julien and Jesus, the ex-leper. This position is used at various points in the story. On the first important hunting expedition Julien kills a wild goat, its companion jumps into a precipice, and Julien, trying to stab it: 'tomba sur le cadavre de l'autre, la face au-dessus de l'abîme et les deux bras écartés' (pp.180–1). When he returns from the second sterile expedition Julien bends over the bed to kiss his wife: 'Alors il sentit contre sa bouche l'impression d'une barbe' (p.185). The result here is that he literally kisses his father, and when later, resolved on suicide, he leans over a fountain to judge its depth and comes face to face with his own mirror image, he mistakes it for his father because of the white beard. The father stag also has a white beard, and it could perhaps be suggested that the *face à face* which is missing, that with the stag itself, is displaced to that with the wild goat. This position is also framed as that of the penitent: 'Il resta, pendant la messe, à plat ventre au milieu du portrail, les bras en croix, et le front dans la poussière' (p. 185). It recurs finally when Julien lies down on the corpse-like leper 'bouche contre bouche, poitrine sur poitrine' and is carried up to heaven 'face à face avec Notre-Seigneur Jésus' (p. 187).

The inevitable conclusion is that Julien is still face to face with his *own* image. The detail that he is 'nu comme au jour de sa naissance' (p. 187), means that the story has come full circle and recalls the comparison of the baby Julien with the infant Jesus. Julien, the leper, and Jesus are all parts of the same figure. From the two opening predictions stem both a saintly and a horrific Julien. The remark 'sa propre personne lui faisait tellement horreur' (p. 186) exactly precedes the introduction of the repulsive leper,[23] and the final merging of all three parts at the end allows an overview of the story as an ambitious experiment in the process of *dédoublement*.

The whole story is most obviously contained (and framed) by the play-off between the title and the closing line. The title announces a legend and a saint's story, while the closing tailpiece repeats this title with a summary of the story: 'Et voilà l'histoire de saint Julien l'Hospitalier, telle à peu près qu'on la trouve, sur un vitrail d'église, dans mon pays' (p. 187). By telling us that the story is contained in a stained glass window, an effect is achieved whereby the story contains the window, but the window contains the story, and so on *ad infinitum*. The window does not play the role of an external source, but joins in a process orientated towards the impossible interior of the story, in the quite literal sense of *mise en abyme*. Indeed, it might stand as an emblem for Flaubert's conception of the literary work. Although belonging to an art-form that, like the written text, needs to be read in a linear manner – panel by panel – it also invites the simultaneous, overall perception so important to Flaubert, and so obviously encouraged by the ending of this tale. The reader will ideally be lulled into a state of reverie by this *opaque* work of art, while the story represented within its stained glass will be distanced into a different ontological dimension.

5

OVERTURNING REALITY

My discussion in chapter 1 of what Sartre means by the 'aesthetic' or 'imaginary' attitude showed that it involves the adoption of a different mode of consciousness whereby what is real is derealized — that is, experienced as if it were being imagined. I noted that there is a problem for Sartre over the evaluation of the aesthetic attitude, since it suggests an unhealthy preference for a particular way of life, yet is the 'normal' way of experiencing a work of art.[1] Looking at Flaubert's behaviour in the Orient we found a good example of the two possible attitudes which might be taken. Maxime Du Camp describes Flaubert as being permanently in a daze and 'not quite there', and Flaubert himself admits to a habitual state of mind resembling that of somebody who has had too much to drink. While for the former this state is negative, for the latter it is clearly something positive, involving a conscious enjoyment of the ability to experience life as a dream.

Those fictional characters whose relationship to reality is abnormal have instant access to the realm of the unreal, and an evaluation of the status of reality in Flaubert's works will reveal another area in which supposedly pathological characters become aesthetically privileged. A dogged undermining of success in the practical world parallels the debunking of superficial eloquence and intelligence already discussed, and sets in relief the preference for extreme passivity that Sartre has analysed so impressively and which is certainly woven into Flaubert's fictional world-view. Not surprisingly this is most obviously spelled out in the heroes of the early works — through the exaggerated autistic characteristics of Djalioh in *Quidquid volueris*, for example, whose plainly intended moral worth has already been analysed: 'il était muet, et son regard ne parlait pas plus que ses lèvres; son œil était de plomb et sa figure était stupide' (I, p. 106); 'c'était, au contraire, la réalité qui l'écrasait' (p. 109).

But art and passivity are linked above all through the character of Jules in the 1845 *L'Éducation sentimentale*.[2] As Sartre claims,

Overturning reality

Jules stands as an empty glorification of the artist, a deliberately pathetic character who has to be a puny failure in order to become an artist at all, a 'nature nerveuse et féminine' (I, p. 308), for whom the later Henry acts as an obvious foil: 'il s'est lancé tout entier dans la vie pratique' (p. 363); 'Savez-vous qu'Henry va faire un riche mariage, un puissant, un superbe mariage? il épouse la nièce d'un ministre, celui dont le fils est son ami; on lui assure deux cent mille francs de dot, il en aura autant plus tard' (p. 373). Jules, on the other hand, leaves the novel for the Orient, taking with him a copy of Homer, an action perhaps included by Flaubert as an allusion to Werther. That the model for Henry is a character from Balzac, and for Jules, Werther or his like, is made apparent in the following extract from a letter:

Les héros pervers de Balzac ont, je crois, tourné la tête à bien des gens. La grêle génération qui s'agite maintenant à Paris, autour du pouvoir et de la renommée, a puisé dans ces lectures l'admiration bête d'une certaine immoralité bourgeoise, à quoi elle s'efforce d'atteindre. J'ai eu des confidences à ce sujet. Ce n'est plus Werther ni Saint-Preux que l'on veut être, mais Rastignac, ou Lucien de Rubempré.

D'ailleurs tous ces fameux gaillards, pratiques, actifs, qui connaissent les hommes, admirent peu l'admiration, visent au solide, font du bruit, se démènent comme des galériens, etc., tous ces malins, dis-je, me font pitié, et au point de vue même de leur malice. *(Corr.* (B) II, p. 440 (1853))

This is a theme developed with far greater subtlety in the 1869 *Éducation* (with Deslauriers as the Balzacian mouthpiece), and I shall demonstrate later in this chapter that, without Frédéric's being an artist figure like Jules, a paradoxically more important aesthetic value is attached to Frédéric's less schematized but equally radical passivity.

Although complete stillness and silence could be seen as morbid features of personality, I have pointed out their positive role in Flaubert's aesthetically slanted system of values. Similarly, other potentially pathological symptoms, avid contemplation or a more docile mode of perception whereby thought becomes strange to itself, are aesthetically important because they seek to preserve the opaqueness and strangeness of the object perceived, and this, as we have seen, appears to be the ideal relationship, based on contemplation, that Flaubert would establish between reader and work of literature.

We therefore find that the many autistic poses and 'stupid' stares of the central characters of the early works – Djalioh, Julietta, Smarh and Saint Antoine[3] – turn through a characteristic 'ébahissement' to aesthetic amazement, and so into a fully developed and ultimately self-conscious aesthetic attitude. In Giacomo's experience of reality as 'une fantasmagorie dont il ne comprenait pas l'énigme' (I, p. 80), and Mazza's of the people in the streets as 'ombres chinoises', reality is already presented as something of a 'spectacle': 'Tout cela lui parut un immense spectacle, un vaste théâtre' (I, p. 119), as is the loss of substantiality of the passing crowd in *Novembre*:

Toutes ces têtes passaient vite devant moi: les unes souriaient, sifflaient en partant, les cheveux au vent; d'autres étaient pâles, d'autres rouges, d'autres livides; elles disparaissaient rapidement à mes côtés, elles glissaient les unes après les autres comme les enseignes lorsqu'on est en voiture. (I, p. 252)[4]

In *Mémoires d'un fou* the narrator is beginning to enjoy his 'hébétement stupide' (I, p. 239), and in *Novembre* 'béance' is accompanied by astonishment rather than unease.[5] In the early Henry of the first *Éducation* both kinds of 'hébétement' are present: a dullness and stupidity caused by the strangeness of his new surroundings, which is depressing and emphasizes his loneliness ('les yeux tout grands ouverts, il contemplait d'un air stupide les quatre pieds de cuivre d'une vieille commode en acajou plaqué qui se trouvait là' (I, p. 278); 'il entrait dans un café et restait une heure entière à lire la même ligne d'un journal' (p. 279)), and, in his affair with Mme Renaud, a stupefied 'enivrement' and 'avidité' of amazed contemplation, which now characterizes enjoyment, and yet shares remarkably similar qualities: 'dans l'enivrement d'eux-mêmes [...] Ils se regardèrent, avides et stupéfaits' (p. 314).[6]

It is strange that in the face of all the evidence for Flaubert's own hatred of active success in the practical world, there should be such widespread belief in Sherrington's claim that Flaubert is accusing characters like Emma, Frédéric and even Salammbô of being 'unwilling or unable to look at facts' (1970, pp. 229–30), of not facing up to reality or seeing the wisdom of accepting life's limitations: 'Flaubert, we must repeat, regarded this unwillingness coolly to examine reality – to "voir les choses comme elles sont" – as a social disease' (p. 169).[7] The problem comes to a head with Emma Bovary, for the evaluation of her status as heroine of the novel depends upon an evaluation of her dissatisfaction with reality. I believe that her dissatisfaction is presented as a positive moral value, and that this being an important theme of the novel, she therefore emerges as a privileged character. But while Flaubert lends his aesthetic support to Emma's world-view, writing into the novel the idea that 'reality' is somehow inferior, her own experience nevertheless remains negative. Though a reversal of the status of the real and the imaginary does take place through Emma, she fails to see the advantages of the life

of the imagination, and does not (or is not allowed to) ⸱
aesthetic attitude to the world.[8] Unlike Frédéric she is ⸱
nor even provided (unlike Félicité in *Un Cœur simple*), wi⸱
sations for her misfortunes in an inner life.

The familiar question of Emma's status as heroine is mo⸱
ly raised by the ambivalence of her presentation, by the problem of
narrative attitude. Do we sympathize with her very real plight (by a
social reading focusing on her class condition, for example),[9] or are
we led either to openly laugh at her or at least to adopt a critical stance
towards her foolish, 'romantic' aspirations, her selfish concern with
herself and her constant histrionic self-dramatization? Both questions
might well be asked. For a large part of the novel we are obliged to share
her viewpoint on the world and on the events of her life, to live through
the reasons for her unhappiness and participate in her depression. At
other points she is suddenly withdrawn from the foreground and her
role as privileged consciousness, the changing viewpoint technique
turning her into an object and introducing an ironic, critical dimension.

A good example of the ambiguity between the two views of Emma
is the Sunday afternoon visit to the flax mill where she is led to contrast Charles with Léon, and comes to realize that she is in love with
the latter. The masterly description of Charles weaves cruel details
('ses deux grosses lèvres tremblotaient') into Emma's perception of
her husband, conveying powerfully to the reader her sense of physical
irritation:

Emma, qui lui donnait le bras, s'appuyait un peu sur son épaule, et elle
regardait le disque du soleil irradiant au loin, dans la brume, sa pâleur
éblouissante; mais elle tourna la tête: Charles était là. Il avait sa casquette
enfoncée sur les sourcils, et ses deux grosses lèvres tremblotaient, ce qui
ajoutait à son visage quelque chose de stupide; son dos même, son dos
tranquille était irritant à voir, et elle y trouvait étalée sur la redingote toute
la platitude du personnage.   (I, p. 608)

The reader is bound to sympathize with Emma, and is far from feeling
sorry for Charles. Yet when we come to her bedtime realization that
Léon loves her, the same cruel details are woven into the presentation
of Emma herself: the slightly affected stretching and pursing of the
lips for a kiss, the sudden intrusion of somewhat declamatory direct
speech, and, worst of all, the equation of a unique and important
moment for Emma with an essentially commonplace experience
('l'éternelle lamentation'):

Elle le trouvait charmant; elle ne pouvait s'en détacher; elle se rappela ses
autres attitudes en d'autres jours, des phrases qu'il avait dites, le son de sa

voix, toute sa personne; et elle répétait, en avançant ses lèvres comme pour un baiser:
— Oui, charmant! charmant! ... N'aime-t-il pas? se demanda-t-elle. Qui donc? ... mais c'est moi!
Toutes les preuves à la fois s'en étalèrent, son cœur bondit. La flamme de la cheminée faisait trembler au plafond une clarté joyeuse; elle se tourna sur le dos en s'étirant les bras.
Alors commença l'éternelle lamentation: 'Oh! si le ciel l'avait voulu! Pourquoi n'est-ce pas? Qui l'empêchait donc? ...'   (p. 609)

One has only to imagine the way an author like Jane Austen (or even Stendhal) would have handled a scene where 'the heroine realizes she is falling in love', to grasp all the difference between an essentially kindly irony and the almost gratuitous cruelty involved in turning Emma into an object for the reader when the delicacies of her inner life are at stake.

The ambivalent presentation is even carried into the representation of her thoughts by Flaubert's famous use of *style indirect libre*. Auerbach's well-known and still powerful analysis of the meal-time scenes at Tostes captures its importance for a positive portrayal of Emma: while the unfolding of her thoughts remains entirely subjective, the subtle narrating interventions turn a vague, ill-defined malaise into a powerful feeling of dissatisfaction, the causes of which can be understood by the reader (1973, p. 488).[10] The passage concerning Emma's desire that her baby should be a boy provokes another good example of the way this works. It begins: 'Elle souhaitait un fils; il serait fort et brun; elle l'appellerait Georges.' This is probably as much as Emma would be directly aware of, yet the text continues:

et cette idée d'avoir pour enfant un mâle était comme la revanche en espoir de toutes ses impuissances passées. Un homme, au moins, est libre; il peut parcourir les passions et les pays, traverser les obstacles, mordre aux bonheurs les plus lointains. Mais une femme est empêchée continuellement. Inerte et flexible à la fois, elle a contre elle les mollesses de la chair avec les dépendances de la loi. Sa volonté, comme le voile de son chapeau retenu par un cordon, palpite à tous les vents, il y a toujours quelque désir qui entraîne, quelque convenance qui retient.   (p. 604)

This clearly goes far beyond the actual thoughts in Emma's mind, developing her own semi-awareness of the disadvantages of being a woman, and in the last sentence introducing a poetic image — the veil of her hat pulled away by the wind and yet still held back — which is obviously contributed by Flaubert and yet still seems worded by Emma herself. And yet, because of its mimetic potential, *style indirect*

libre is also a way of introducing a strong note of iron
the reader from becoming completely and uncritically
her consciousness. Consider, for instance, the effect of
tion mark in 'elle valait bien, cependant, toutes celle;
heureuses!' (p. 597), or a far more cruel example: the
exclamation mark of '(elle qui était si intelligente!)' (p. 637), which
transform an innocent piece of *style indirect libre* into a severely
negative evaluation of the speaker, though the reader is certainly
otherwise made to enter into Emma's nervously bitter and dogged
reasoning:

> Comment donc avait-elle fait (elle qui était si intelligente!) pour se méprendre
> encore une fois? Du reste, par quelle déplorable manie avoir ainsi abîmé son
> existence en sacrifices continuels? Elle se rappela tous ses instincts de luxe,
> toutes les privations de son âme, les bassesses du mariage, du ménage, ses
> rêves tombant dans la boue comme des hirondelles blessées, tout ce qu'elle
> avait désiré, tout ce qu'elle s'était refusé, tout ce qu'elle aurait pu avoir! Et
> pourquoi? pourquoi? (p. 637)

The climax of this almost sadistic treatment of Emma is the famous
example of the cab ride with Léon, analysed so well by Sartre (*L'Idiot*
II, pp. 1275–86). One has only to recall the more delicate seduction
scenes in Flaubert (the lyrical forest scene with Rodolphe, the tent
scene in *Salammbô*, the first kiss in *Un Cœur simple*),[11] to grasp the
full import of what Flaubert chooses to do to our view of Emma here.

Nevertheless, as I have already suggested, it is possible to move
beyond the tension between the sympathy with her viewpoint to which
the text invites us, and the overall ironic treatment of her silliness.
For there is a tendency towards a more fundamental sympathy of
mind, which goes beyond superficial sympathy or criticism, constituting a serious view of Emma's experience. If Emma is dissatisfied
with her life and with reality, it is reality which is blamed, not Emma,
however unintelligent she may be. Written into her story is the suggestion that although her hopes and dreams almost inevitably wither
into lies and disappointments, this is only marginally Emma's fault,
for there is something fundamentally wrong with the reality which
cannot meet her needs. In other words, despite her silliness, her
metaphysical unease is taken seriously. She is the only character in
the novel to feel it, except perhaps for the *perruquier* at Tostes whom
she watches through her window at the height of her depression, and
the nature of whose dreams indicate his specific relationship to Emma:

> Lui aussi, le perruquier, il se lamentait de sa vocation arrêtée, de son avenir
> perdu, et, rêvant quelque boutique *dans une grande ville, comme à Rouen,*

par exemple, sur le port, près du théâtre, il restait toute la journée à se promener en long, depuis la mairie jusqu'à l'église, sombre, et attendant la clientèle. (p. 596, my emphasis)

It is not just that her convent education has given her aspirations 'above her station', or that she has read too many novels and as a consequence expects too much from life and love. In fact Flaubert typically and self-consciously problematizes this theme, by turning 'the dangers of reading too many novels' into a cliché, and putting it into the mouth of Emma's mother-in-law:

— Sais-tu ce qu'il faudrait à ta femme? reprenait la mère Bovary. Ce seraient des occupations forcées, des ouvrages manuels! Si elle était, comme tant d'autres, contrainte à gagner son pain, elle n'aurait pas ces vapeurs-là, qui lui viennent d'un tas d'idées qu'elle se fourre dans la tête, et du désœuvrement où elle vit.

— Pourtant elle s'occupe, disait Charles.

— Ah! elle s'occupe! A quoi donc? A lire des romans, de mauvais livres, des ouvrages qui sont contre la religion et dans lesquels on se moque des prêtres par des discours tirés de Voltaire. Mais tout cela va loin, mon pauvre enfant, et quelqu'un qui n'a pas de religion finit toujours par tourner mal.

Donc, il fut résolu que l'on empêcherait Emma de lire des romans. L'entreprise ne semblait point facile. La bonne dame s'en chargea: elle devait, quand elle passerait par Rouen, aller en personne chez le loueur de livres et lui représenter qu'Emma cessait ses abonnements. N'aurait-on pas le droit d'avertir la police, si le libraire persistait quand même dans son métier d'empoisonneur? (p. 617)

It is impossible to align Flaubert himself with the view satirized here. This view is presented as an even more pertinent commonplace in the drafts, where the mother-in-law declares to Homais: 'car ces livres, dont vous parlez, font voir l'existence en beau; puis quand on arrive à la réalité, on trouve du désenchantement' (Pommier and Leleu, 1949, p. 327). The irony of this is picked up later in the final version: 'd'abord Charles n'avait point écouté ses conseils pour l'interdiction des romans' (I, p. 639). The end effect of this ambivalence is well summed up by Rainer Warning:

if he thus ironizes the Romantic model, he nonetheless retains the book-hating mother-in-law, with whom that irony is in turn ironized. The theme of the harmful effects of reading novels does not remain, as Culler supposes, an 'island of certainty' but rather is ironized by means of the alternative of a threatened 'prohibition of novels'. This book-hating mother-in-law, this 'scandalized bourgeoisie' [...] becomes the instrument by which the tables are turned again, and Emma, with her hunger for books, and her subscription book-dealer in Rouen are vindicated anew. (1982, p. 280)

The two sides of the problem are further explored in the account of Emma's visit to the opera. Emma has just forged for herself a notion of art as 'une fantaisie plastique bonne à abuser les yeux', when she falls victim to the illusion created by Lagardy, and the scene culminates in a near hallucination that it is she whom he addresses:

> Elle connaissait à présent la petitesse des passions que l'art exagérait. S'efforçant donc d'en détourner sa pensée, Emma voulait ne plus voir dans cette reproduction de ses douleurs qu'une fantaisie plastique bonne à abuser les yeux et même elle souriait intérieurement d'une pitié dédaigneuse quand, au fond du théâtre, sous la portière de velours, un homme apparut en manteau noir.
>
> [...] Il devait avoir, pensait-elle, un intarissable amour, pour en déverser sur la foule à si larges effluves. Toutes ses velléités de dénigrement s'évanouissaient sous la poésie du rôle qui l'envahissait, et, entraînée vers l'homme par l'illusion du personnage, elle tâcha de se figurer sa vie, cette vie retentissante, extraordinaire, splendide, et qu'elle aurait pu mener, cependant, si le hasard l'avait voulu. Ils se seraient connus, ils se seraient aimés! [...] de la scène, tout en jouant, il l'aurait regardée. Mais une folie la saisit; il la regardait, c'est sûr! Elle eut envie de courir dans ses bras pour se réfugier en sa force.
>
> (I, pp. 650–1)

The curtain falls on Emma's fantasy, but ironically this scene immediately precedes the reappearance of Léon, with whom Emma will attempt once more to play out the fantasy in her own more mediocre life. However, the irony is directed not so much at her longing for an extraordinary and splendid existence, but more at her gross misunderstanding of the workings of art,[12] whereby she confuses the dramatic illusion of the character with the actor himself.

Nor does Flaubert present Emma as a straightforward victim of mediocre surroundings and a stifling bourgeois society, for if he paints a satirical portrait of the deadly inhabitants of Yonville, Emma's short-lived flights from their company into a more spiritual realm are shown up as suspect.[13] It is Emma's own mistake to blame the immediate circumstances of her life, to think it is her boring native farm, then Tostes and her marriage, then Yonville that are holding her back. By placing Emma in different surroundings Flaubert hammers home the lesson that the environment makes no difference, that all real experience is equally sterile. Emma herself only grasps this idea that it is life itself which is at fault, and not just her situation, as she sits on a bench outside her old convent at Rouen, towards the end of her story. Reliving memorable moments of her past, she suddenly finds Léon, whom she has just left, as distant as all the other men:

— Je l'aime pourtant! se disait-elle.

N'importe! elle n'était pas heureuse, ne l'avait jamais été. D'où venait donc cette insuffisance de la vie, cette pourriture instantanée des choses où elle s'appuyait?... Mais, s'il y avait quelque part un être fort et beau, une nature valeureuse, pleine à la fois d'exaltation et de raffinements, un cœur de poète sous une forme d'ange, lyre aux cordes d'airain, sonnant vers le ciel des épithalames élégiaques, pourquoi, par hasard, ne le trouverait-elle pas? Oh! quelle impossibilité! Rien, d'ailleurs, ne valait la peine d'une recherche; tout mentait! Chaque sourire cachait un bâillement d'ennui, chaque joie une malédiction, tout plaisir son dégoût, et les meilleurs baisers ne vous laissent sur la lèvre qu'une irréalisable envie d'une volupté plus haute. (p. 670)

The old definitions of *bovarysme* as a condition in which we delude ourselves as to what we are and as to life's potential (Gaultier, 1921), would surely be better recast as the condition of 'knowing life's potential and refusing to be satisfied with it'. Where Emma falls short of redemption by way of the aesthetic attitude to her experience is in failing to grasp that the insight 'tout mentait!' could be positive. This is something that Flaubert himself suggests through his presentation of Emma's experience, but that she herself never integrates into her own world-view.

Emma's rejection of her everyday experience in favour of dreams and anticipation is the character trait for which she is famous. It is only the faraway, imaginary existence that seems real to her; the nearer things are, the more quickly they wither into nothingness. A reversal of the real and the imaginary takes place as a climax to Emma's furious reverie during the amputation scene:

Le souvenir de son amant revenait à elle avec des attractions vertigineuses; elle y jetait son âme, emportée vers cette image par un enthousiasme nouveau; et Charles lui semblait aussi détaché de sa vie, aussi absent pour toujours, aussi impossible et anéanti que s'il allait mourir et qu'il eût agonisé sous ses yeux. (p. 637)

In an early draft for the parallel descriptions of the Bovarys' nighttime dreams, Emma's attachment to Rodolphe's image was even strong enough to destroy her own sense of reality:

Pour ressaisir quelque chose de ce qui la charmait tout à l'heure, elle tâchait donc de penser à Rodolphe si bien que cette image, peu à peu se rapprochant, lui apparaissait aussi précise que dans la réalité. Alors il semblait à Emma, que tout échappée d'elle-même, elle circulait autour de lui comme un souffle impalpable et qu'elle n'existait plus, tant la conscience de son être se perdait sous cette contemplation. (Pommier and Leleu, 1949, p. 384)

Overturning reality

At two points in the novel Emma does succeed in taking something like the aesthetic attitude to herself, as Claude Perruchot, in a brief intervention at the Cerisy colloquium, subtly suggests (Gothot-Mersch, 1975, pp. 428–9). The first is the moment at La Vaubyessard when a servant breaks two window panes to let in some air, and Emma sees the faces of the peasants looking in at the ball. Though this view at first causes her to resee herself on her father's farm, the more crucial significance of the missing panes is that Emma is thereby framed for those looking in:

Mais aux fulgurations de l'heure présente, sa vie passée, si nette jusqu'alors, s'évanouissait tout entière, et elle doutait presque de l'avoir vécue. Elle était là; puis autour du bal, il n'y avait plus que de l'ombre, étalée sur tout le reste. Elle mangeait alors une glace au marasquin, qu'elle tenait de la main gauche dans une coquille de vermeil, et fermait à demi les yeux, la cuiller entre les dents. (p. 592)

It is only in the eyes of the peasants looking in that Emma, half-shutting her own eyes over the maraschino ice, attains her imaginary identity, a recognition conveyed by Flaubert's use of the free indirect phrase: 'elle était là'. Perruchot describes this as a 'manière d'*être là*, en représentation seulement et dans un présent déjà creusé du futur antérieur d'une inscription possible' (Gothot-Mersch, 1975, p. 429). Referring to the 'allure fuyante du cheval noir platonicien', he also suggests that when Emma gazes at herself in her mirror on her return from the first ride with Rodolphe, the mirror serves to contest her repeated 'J'ai un amant!' (I, p. 629) with an implicitly understood 'J'aurai eu un amant.' Indeed the text goes on to state that she manages to fuse herself with an artistic representation:

Alors elle se rappela les héroïnes des livres qu'elle avait lus, et la légion lyrique de ces femmes adultères se mit à chanter dans sa mémoire avec des voix de sœurs qui la charmaient. Elle devenait elle-même comme une partie véritable de ces imaginations et réalisait la longue rêverie de sa jeunesse, en se considérant dans ce type d'amoureuse qu'elle avait tant envié. (p. 629)

But Emma is unable to maintain this position in the face of reality. So, for example, in the first period of their acquaintance at Yonville, Emma prefers the thought of Léon to his actual presence:

Elle était amoureuse de Léon, et elle recherchait la solitude, afin de pouvoir plus à l'aise se délecter en son image. La vue de sa personne troublait la volupté de cette méditation. Emma palpitait au bruit de ses pas, puis, en sa présence, l'émotion tombait, et il ne lui restait ensuite qu'un immense étonnement qui se finissait en tristesse. (p. 610)[14]

This is an example of the almost common reversal of the real and the imaginary, with stress on the inferiority of reality. But this preference for irreality, this voluptuous lingering over an image, is not made positive for Emma, in that it is spoiled by the return to reality that Léon's arrival represents.

To convey Emma's rare moments of extreme pleasure, Flaubert creates a seeming fusion between her state of mind and her surroundings, through delicate descriptions of the natural world and of blissful moments of silence. Such lyricism is carried into the presentation of Emma's dreams and reveries, where free indirect narration of her fantasies lends them a spurious air of reality. This is fostered by a confusion of two separate imperfect tenses: that of the *style indirect libre* by means of which Emma's thoughts are recounted, and that by which repeated occurences are described. Thus the imaginary events of Emma's dreams are not readily distinguishable from some descriptions of real events — indeed, the reader might well be 'fooled' for several lines. Take for example the episode in which Emma and Charles lie beside each other in bed, each dreaming different dreams of the future. While Charles's dreams of Berthe growing up into a second Emma are described in the conditional tense: 'elle porterait, comme elle [...] de grands chapeaux de paille! [...] elle lui broderait des pantoufles', Emma's more fantastic dreams are both introduced ('elle se réveillait en d'autres rêves') and then described in the imperfect:

Au galop de quatre chevaux, elle était emportée depuis huit jours vers un pays nouveau [...] Ils allaient, ils allaient, les bras enlacés, sans parler. Souvent, du haut d'une montagne, ils apercevaient tout à coup quelque cité splendide avec des dômes, des ponts, des navires, des forêts de citronniers et des cathédrales de marbre blanc, dont les clochers aigus portaient des nids de cigogne. On marchait au pas à cause des grandes dalles, et il y avait par terre des bouquets de fleurs que vous offraient des femmes habillées en rouge [...] Et puis ils arrivaient, un soir, dans un village de pêcheurs, où des filets bruns séchaient au vent, le long de la falaise et des cabanes. (pp. 640–1)

Despite its geographical vagueness and clichéd aspects, the extraordinary detail of this evocation of what is supposed to be only a recurrent nightly dream (sustained for nearly a page), makes this passage seem like a description of real events. Indeed, Emma's visions are frequently, by tense and degree of detail, conveyed with *more* conviction than real events, and this is an important way in which Flaubert lends his technical skills, as well as his intellectual and moral support, to Emma's preference for the unreal.

Surely, therefore, it trivializes the novel as a whole to consider Emma simply deluded, a woman who has read too much and comes to a bad end − a 'case-history of frustration' (Thorlby, 1956, p. 40) − however much those who make such claims may admire the way the novel is written.[15] Flaubert's choice of a mediocre vehicle in Emma is a deliberate and positive one. His wager is precisely the decision to create an unintelligent woman as the mouthpiece for a serious world-view, and this is what gives the actual story of *Madame Bovary* its interest. The theme of lost illusions and of dissatisfaction with the world is common enough in modern literature, but what is different here is that the heroine's suffering and sense of aloneness are not at all compensated for by a sense of moral superiority: compare Julien Sorel, so much a stranger to his environment and even to his century, yet so intelligent, so talented, and so much an exceptional being. It is not just a case of choosing a central character from a nondescript background, but of inventing a rather silly woman, and then of allowing her to carry one branch of the moral weight of the novel.

In comparison with Emma's, Frédéric Moreau's maladjustment to reality is both more extreme yet more positive. This is partly because Frédéric's own evaluation of the merits of an active life is so different from Emma's. Flaubert's allusion to the popularity of Balzac's Rastignac and de Rubempré as models for living − as opposed to Goethe's Werther and Rousseau's Saint-Preux − spells out how explicitly Frédéric is conceived as an anti-Rastignac, who is ironically caught up in a society where all the pressures and values are 'Balzacian'. In the opening chapter Frédéric has been sent to visit his uncle to attempt to secure the inheritance that will give him an important future, but he falls in love with Mme Arnoux instead, on the very same journey. Already his own values conflict with those of his mother, as their conversation that closes the first chapter makes clear:

— Eh bien?
Le vieillard l'avait reçu très cordialement, mais sans montrer ses intentions.
Mme Moreau soupira.
'Où est-elle, à présent?' songeait-il.   (II, p. 12)

Frédéric's attitude to life is summed up in his declaration to Mme Arnoux: 'Qu'est-ce que j'ai à faire dans le monde? Les autres s'évertuent pour la richesse, la célébrité, le pouvoir! Moi, je n'ai pas d'état, vous êtes mon occupation exclusive, toute ma fortune, le but, le centre de mon existence, de mes pensées' (p. 106).

Nor is it the case that Frédéric prefers the thought of Mme Arnoux to the reality of her presence. Indeed he is able to build up and sustain an imaginary relationship through that very presence. This is evident in his first view of her: 'Ce fut comme une apparition' (p. 9). Mme Arnoux is real but Frédéric perceives her as if she were an image. This fusion is fostered by the happy coincidence with a literary model that is referred to in the text: 'Elle ressemblait aux femmes des livres romantiques. Il n'aurait voulu rien ajouter, rien retrancher à sa personne' (p. 11). Flaubert's rough notes for the novel establish the importance for the future course of Frédéric's passion of this initial coincidence of the real with an imaginary ideal: 'violence que doit avoir un amour renforcé par des types littéraires admirés dans la jeunesse − il y a coincidence de l'idéal & du Réel'.[16] Not only is the whole nature of the relationship defined by Frédéric's original perception of Mme Arnoux in what corresponds to Sartre's aesthetic attitude, but his own perceiving self undergoes a corresponding loss of substance. Frédéric exactly fits Sartre's claim that, for the construction of an image always to be possible, consciousness must possess the capacity for positing a hypothesis of unreality, must be able, that is, to escape from the world by its very nature. Like Sartre's actor who feels in an 'unreal' way, who sacrifices his own reality so that an appearance can exist, Frédéric exists in a permanently derealized state which maintains the 'real' Mme Arnoux as an image.

An allusion to Werther is woven into the famous scene of Frédéric's last meeting with Mme Arnoux: 'Je comprends les Werther que ne dégoûtent pas les tartines de Charlotte' (p. 160). The reference is a crucial one. The nature of Frédéric's own obsession, its origin and its effect on his manner of existing in the world, very closely resembles that described by Werther in his declaration to Lotte: 'Ah, how I attached myself to you from the first moment and could not let go'; 'Since then [...] the world around me has vanished' (Goethe, 1962, pp. 126 and 41). The way in which Frédéric's total self-investment in an unknown image turns him into an artist is superbly glossed by parts of Barthes's simulated discourse of the romantic lover. Nor is it simply a coincidence that Barthes's *Fragments d'un discours amoureux* should be so directly applicable to Frédéric as neurotic lover. On the one hand, Barthes's text is full of echoes of Sartre's *L'Imaginaire*, which already provides an important conceptual framework for understanding Frédéric. On the other, the archetypal Werther, to whom Frédéric is so clearly related, is the object of Barthes's most sustained commentary:

Descendant de voiture, Werther voit pour la première fois Charlotte (dont il s'éprend), encadrée par la porte de sa maison (elle coupe des tartines aux enfants: scène célèbre, souvent commentée): nous aimons d'abord *un tableau*. Car il faut au coup de foudre le signe même de sa soudaineté (qui me fait irresponsable, soumis à la fatalité, emporté, ravi): et, de tous les arrangements d'objets, c'est le tableau qui semble le mieux se voir pour la première fois: un rideau se déchire: ce qui n'avait été encore jamais vu est découvert dans son entité, et dès lors, dévoré des yeux: l'immédiat vaut pour le plein: je suis initié: le tableau *consacre* l'objet que je vais aimer. (p. 227)

je ne cesse de m'étonner d'avoir eu cette chance: rencontrer ce qui va à mon désir; ou d'avoir pris ce risque énorme: m'asservir d'un coup à une image inconnue. (p. 229)

Flaubert describes Frédéric as immediately seized, at the sight of Mme Arnoux, with something more than a desire for physical possession: 'une envie plus profonde [...] une curiosité qui n'avait pas de limites' (II, p. 10). He enters into an infinite ecstasy of contemplation embracing everything associated with Mme Arnoux, attaching himself to her very ordinariness. Flaubert's prized quality of amazement before the work of art is so evident in Frédéric's perceptions, that it actually turns Mme Arnoux and her belongings into opaque 'works of art':

Il considérait son panier à ouvrage avec ébahissement, comme une chose extraordinaire. (p. 10)

Il ne parlait guère pendant ces dîners; il la contemplait [...] son peigne, ses gants, ses bagues étaient pour lui des choses particuliers, importantes comme des œuvres d'art. (p. 28)

We have already seen that a chance meeting in the street with Mme Arnoux has all the qualities of an amazing adventure, and when she happens to call at his house, it is 'un événement extraordinaire, presque une bonne fortune' (p. 76). When he accompanies her on an errand in the smelly fog: 'Frédéric le humait avec délices ... il lui semblait qu'ils étaient tous les deux comme bercés par le vent, au milieu d'un nuage' (p. 33), and the memory of this, on a similar walk with Rosanette, makes the absent Mme Arnoux seem more real than the present Rosanette: 'Alors il se rappela un crépuscule d'hiver, où, sur le même trottoir, Mme Arnoux marchait ainsi à son côté; et ce souvenir l'absorbait tellement, qu'il ne s'apercevait plus de Rosanette et n'y songeait pas' (p. 63). The walk in the fog is reminiscent of Flaubert's meeting with the caravan in the Egyptian desert, and the memory of it shows how easily Frédéric's imagination can dominate reality, for his daydreams are apt to produce hallucinations: 'Et sa rêverie devint tellement profonde, qu'il eut une sorte d'hallucination' (p. 139). When Frédéric considers suicide, he has a morbid hallucination of his body floating in the river, and, before his duel with Cisy, another of his mother in mourning. But more often this tendency to hallucinate is both positive and creative.[17]

Flaubert invariably lends these versions the same aesthetic support as Emma's: through tense and degree of detail they are given the concreteness of 'real' fictional events. Consider the following examples:

La diligence roul*ait*, et, enveloppé dans le châle *sans doute*, elle appuy*ait* contre le drap du coupé sa belle tête endormie.   (p. 12)

Elle *était* en chemin de fer, *sans doute*, le visage au carreau du wagon [...] Puis il la voyait dans une chambre d'auberge, avec des malles par terre, un papier de tenture en lambeaux, la porte qui trembl*ait* au vent.

(p. 156, my emphases)

Only the careful insertion of a delayed 'sans doute' distinguishes these fantasies from descriptions of real actions, while the details of the wallpaper and the door are extremely delicate ones for an imaginary sequence. During the first river journey Frédéric imagines himself walking with Mme Arnoux in the surrounding countryside, a fantasy linked by the detail of the yellowing leaves to their autumnal love affair at Auteuil: 'Quel bonheur de monter côte à côte, le bras autour de sa taille, pendant que sa robe balayerait les feuilles jaunies, en écoutant sa voix, sous le rayonnement de ses yeux!' (pp. 10–11). Then, as the boat passes a château, Frédéric's dream is reflected in a rapidly glimpsed tableau: 'Il se la figura passant au bord des chamilles. A ce moment, une jeune dame et un jeune homme se montrèrent sur le perron, entre les caisses d'oranger. Puis tout disparut' (p. 11). The sudden appearance of the couple, and the equally sudden disappearance of the whole scene, give to this brief description the quality of a hallucination, but it is presumably to be taken, this time, as a real event.[18]

When Frédéric hears about his inheritance he sees himself, 'avec la netteté d'une hallucination', delivering a present to Mme Arnoux: 'tandis qu'à la porte stationnerait son tilbury, non, un coupé plutôt! un coupé noir, avec un domestique en livrée brune' (p. 43). He is clearly 'working' on the details here, and later in the same episode he is compared with an architect in his mental arrangement of his life (p. 44). When he does National Guard duty with Arnoux, and imagines Arnoux dead and himself living with his widow: 'Il s'arrêtait même à des calculs de ménage, des dispositions domestiques, contemplant, palpant déjà son bonheur', and here we are told that he 's'étendit sur cette idée, comme un dramaturge qui compose' (p. 123). In cases like these the inwardness of the contemplation cannot be seen as passive, but the price for this creativity seems to be loss of the sense of reality of the rest of the world and of Frédéric himself. In the first example just quoted his contemplation is so profound 'que les objets extérieurs avaient disparu' (p. 44), and in the second 'dans la fureur de sa rêverie, le reste du monde s'effaçait; et il n'avait conscience de lui-même que par un intolérable serrement à la poitrine' (p. 123). An early descrip-tion of Léon's attitude to Emma acts as an appropriate comment upon Frédéric's to Mme Arnoux:

À force de se renouveler, son émotion donc s'affaiblit ou elle s'immobilisa plutôt. Madame Bovary devint pour sa pensée une aventure permanente [...] Les autres objets du monde flottaient confondus comme des brumes matinales dans un soleil levant, et sa propre conscience même semblait l'abandonner, tant elle se penchait tout entière, en dehors de lui, sur cette contemplation.
(Pommier and Leleu, 1949, pp. 275–6)

All the features of derealization described in my original account of aesthetic contemplation are present here, and recall Sartre's emphasis on the vicious circle of 'unrealities' into which the artist must necessarily enter. The passage also recalls Flaubert's distinction between the different relationships to reality in the artistic and the psychotic hallucination: in the *first* the real world disappears.

Frédéric is never properly integrated into the events around him, as in the well-known example in which he experiences the sacking of the Palais Royal as a 'spectacle': 'Les blessés qui tombaient, les morts étendus n'avaient pas l'air de vrais blessés, de vrais morts. Il lui semblait assister à un spectacle' (p. 112). For Barthes this is an essential attribute of the romantic and passionate lover: 'Tout ce qui amuse les autres, leurs conversations, leurs passions, leurs indignations, tout ça lui paraît dé-réel. Son "réel" à lui, c'est son rapport à l'objet aimé, et les mille incidents qui le traversent' (1980, p. 280). Barthes defines 'dé-réalité' as 'sentiment de l'absence, retrait de réalité éprouvé par le sujet amoureux, face au monde' (1977, p. 103). He goes on to make a distinc-tion which allows us to evaluate Frédéric's relationship with reality. This distinction is that between the 'irréel', experienced by the happy lover, and the 'déréel', whereby the world is perceived as hostile:

Mais, parfois, la mauvaise humeur épuisée, je n'ai plus aucun langage: le monde n'est pas 'irréel' (je pourrais alors le parler: il y a des arts de l'irréel, et des plus grands), mais déréel: le réel en a fui, nulle part, en sorte que je n'ai plus aucun sens (aucun paradigme) à ma disposition.   (pp. 105–6)

Tantôt le monde est *irréel* (je le parle différemment), tantôt il est *déréel* (je le parle avec peine). Ce n'est pas (dit-on) le même retrait de la réalité. Dans le premier cas, le refus que j'oppose à la réalité se prononce à travers une *fantaisie*: tout mon entour change de valeur par rapport à une fonction, qui est l'Imaginaire; l'amoureux se sépare alors du monde, il l'irréalise parce qu'il fantasme d'un côté les péripéties ou les utopies de son amour; il se livre à l'Image, par rapport à quoi tout 'réel' le dérange. Dans le second cas, je perds aussi le réel, mais aucune substitution imaginaire ne vient compenser cette perte [...] je ne suis même plus dans l'Imaginaire. Tout est figé, pétrifié, immuable, c'est-à-dire *insubstituable*: l'imaginaire est (passagèrement) forclos. Dans le premier moment, je suis névrosé, j'irréalise; dans le second moment, je suis fou, je déréalise.   (pp. 106–7)[19]

The 'déréel' seems to be psychotic, and to fit Sartre's category of those who prefer an impoverished mode of existence. Frédéric rarely approaches this state, except perhaps in his extreme depression after his 'rejection' by Mme Arnoux at Creil, where his loss of reality leads him to 'se laisser pousser' into a railway carriage, in which he promptly falls asleep (II, p. 81). But an investment in the 'irréel' is only neurotic, and parallels the ideal relationship with the work of art.

In the first *Éducation*, at one stage in his love for Mme Renaud, Henry wishes that 'toute sa vie, en un mot, eût été comme une mélodie secrète et particulière qu'il eût composée avec ses mains' (I, p. 324). This may remind us sharply of Swann's 'imaginary' love for Odette, in Proust's *Un Amour de Swann*, where Swann is established as a 'near miss' artist, in that he finally writes off his love as so much wasted effort. Proust's intention, illustrated in the following very specific references to writing, seems remarkably close to that of Flaubert for Frédéric's love for Mme Arnoux, even though Flaubert does not seek to involve Frédéric himself in its writing down:

La petite phrase continuait à s'associer pour Swann à l'amour qu'il avait pour Odette. Il sentait bien que cet amour, c'était quelque chose qui ne correspondait à rien d'extérieur, de constatable par d'autres que lui; il se rendait compte que les qualités d'Odette ne justifiaient pas qu'il attachât tant de prix aux moments passés près d'elle. Et souvent, quand c'était l'intelligence positive qui régnait seule en Swann, il voulait cesser de sacrifier tant d'intérêts intellectuels et sociaux à ce plaisir imaginaire. Mais la petite phrase, dès qu'il l'entendait, savait rendre libre en lui l'espace qui pour elle était nécessaire, les proportions de l'âme de Swann s'en trouvaient changées; une marge y était réservée à une jouissance qui elle non plus ne correspondait à aucun objet extérieur et qui pourtant, au lieu d'être purement individuelle comme celle de l'amour, s'imposait à Swann comme une réalité supérieure aux choses concrètes. Cette soif d'un charme inconnu, la petite phrase l'éveillait en lui, mais ne lui apportait rien de précis pour l'assouvir. De sorte que ces parties de l'âme de Swann où la petite phrase avait effacé le souci des intérêts matériels, les considérations humaines et valables pour tous, elle les avait laissées vacantes et en blanc, et il était libre d'y inscrire le nom d'Odette.

(1954, pp. 282–3)

But though Frédéric is not a writer, he might be viewed metaphorically as a collaborator in Flaubert's creation of a fiction. In his final meeting with Mme Arnoux Frédéric precisely underlines the imaginary nature of their relationship, in claiming that: 'Je n'imaginais rien au-delà. C'était Mme Arnoux telle que vous étiez, avec ses deux enfants, tendre, sérieuse, belle à éblouir, et si bonne! Cette image-là effaçait toutes les autres' (II, p. 161). The self-consciously aesthetic qualities of this last encounter, the 'ils se racontèrent leurs anciens jours', their use of the future anterior ('nous nous serons bien aimés' and 'Quel bonheur nous aurions eu!'), Mme Arnoux's 'il me semble que vous êtes là, quand je lis des passages d'amour dans les livres' (p. 160), are present throughout their relationship, always suffused with this tendency to turn life into a fiction.[20]

This is nowhere more evident than in the description of the repeated meetings at Auteuil, the nearest they come to a consummation of their love, in which genuine ecstasy emerges through ritual and repetition (pp. 106–7). The mood of these meetings is established by the convention that, although they could not possibly be disturbed by unwelcome visitors, they will not belong to each other. Their conversations revolve around the years of their acquaintance:

Il lui rappelait d'insignifiants détails, la couleur de sa robe à telle époque, quelle personne un jour était survenue, ce qu'elle avait dit une autre fois; et elle répondait tout émerveillée:
— Oui, je me rappelle!
Leurs goûts, leurs jugements étaient les mêmes. Souvent celui des deux qui écoutait l'autre s'écriait:
— Moi aussi!
Et l'autre à son tour reprenait:
— Moi aussi! (p. 107)

Remembering, sharing tastes, echoing each other, is turned into an enjoyable game, with accompanying ritualistic elaboration:

— Pourquoi le ciel ne l'a-t-il pas voulu! Si nous nous étions rencontrés! ...
— Ah! si j'avais été plus jeune! soupirait-elle.
— Non! moi un peu plus vieux.
Et ils s'imaginaient une vie exclusivement amoureuse.

91

This sort of thing happens each time; the encounters always follow a controlled pattern. To increase this ritualistic aspect they exchange gifts and give each other special names. Finally they eliminate the surprise element in the timing of Frédéric's visits; Mme Arnoux can now go and meet him each time at the same spot, and throughout the whole period she always wears the same dress. In this ecstasy of repetition: 'le charme de sa personne lui troublait le cœur plus que les sens. C'était une béatitude indéfinie, un tel enivrement, qu'il en oubliait jusqu'à la possibilité d'un bonheur absolu.' In one of the drafts this is nevertheless a sort of possession: 'Il la désirait de loin, plus violemment que de près. Car il la possédait en qq sorte... il éprouvait en sa présence une béatitude exquise' (B.N. n.a.fr. 17606, fol. 130ʳ). Of course the piquancy of the game really comes from the underlying sexual *trouble*: 'Par l'exercice d'un tel mensonge, leur sensibilité s'exaspéra'. The *trouble* is in fact transferred to nature: 'Ils jouissaient délicieusement de la senteur des feuilles humides', and at the slightest sound they are terrified as if they had been guilty. Mme Arnoux on each occasion accuses herself of being a 'coquette' and begs Frédéric not to visit her any more; he, each time, 'répétait les mêmes serments − qu'elle écoutait chaque fois avec plaisir'.

This love therefore remains unconsummated not because the characters conceive of it as a Platonic love, or simply because Frédéric is too weak to act, but because, although the attraction is physical and sexual, it is derealized in the aesthetic attitude. Indeed one could say that Flaubert overmotivates Frédéric's failure to sleep with Mme Arnoux with a mixture of psychological and circumstantial factors. The Auteuil drafts in particular reveal some confusion over Flaubert's conception of their psychological state at this point, and even of the nature of the relationship, which is referred to as 'l'adultère platonique' (n.a.fr. 17611, fol. 106ʳ) and 'l'adultère sans l'adultère' (fol. 40ʳ). The constant danger is part of the game, and it is Mme Arnoux who deliberately introduces it into their final meeting, by her manner of revealing that she had been hiding when Frédéric called with the money:

Alors, d'une voix tremblante, et avec de longs intervalles entre les mots:
— J'avais peur! Oui... peur de vous... de moi!
Cette révélation lui donna comme un saisissement de volupté. Son cœur battit à grands coups. (p. 160)[21]

As Jeanne Bem claims, discussing another pseudo-physical scene, the quarrel over the cashmere shawl (II, pp. 68−9):[22] 'Quand le non-être est conçu comme supérieur, il ne faut surtout pas le faire passer à l'être' (1981, p. 32). The delicate balance between real and imaginary is so nearly destroyed at the last meeting that there is almost a note of insincerity in Mme Arnoux's final: 'Elle le contemplait, tout émerveillée. — Comme vous êtes délicat! Il n'y a que vous! Il n'y a que vous!' (II, p. 161). It is time for the game to stop, and it is appropriate that the image of Mme Arnoux should be abolished with the same magical stroke with which it appeared: 'Et ce fut tout.'

This image is even *framed* for Frédéric and the reader since the last view of her is presented through the open window, as she climbs into a carriage and moves out of the picture: 'Quand elle fut sortie, Frédéric ouvrit sa fenêtre. Mme Arnoux, sur le trottoir, fit signe d'avancer à un fiacre qui passait. Elle monta dedans. La voiture disparut' (p. 161). This final framing of Mme Arnoux underlines her function (for Frédéric and the reader) as an artistic representation, in that it quite literally turns her into a picture. Early on in the novel Frédéric already mentally replaces the portraits in the Louvre with one of Mme Arnoux: 'Coiffée d'un hennin, elle priait à deux genoux derrière un vitrage de plomb' (p. 33). Flaubert merges his own representation of Mme Arnoux with Frédéric's perception of her by very frequently describing her in static tableau form, often framed by effects of light or shadow:

Le regard tourné vers les cendres et une main sur l'épaule du petit garçon, elle défaisait, de l'autre, le lacet de la brassière: le mioche en chemise pleurait tout en se grattant la tête, comme M. Alexandre fils.　　　　　　(p. 47)

et, comme Mme Arnoux était assise auprès de la fenêtre, un grand rayon, frappant les accroche-cœur de sa nuque, pénétrait d'un fluide d'or sa peau ambrée.　　　　　　(p. 57)

Et elle se tenait debout, sur le seuil de sa chambre, avec ses deux enfants à ses côtés.　　　　　　(p. 81)

Indeed there is a striking incidence of explicit, pictorial frames throughout Flaubert's work, emphasizing the link between, on the one hand, characters' abilities to derealize themselves and the objects of their attention by grasping them as a represented image, and, on the other, Flaubert's own preferred (and foregrounded) manner of representing his characters. The characteristic pose of Emma by a window, which has often been noted and is normally given a symbolic or psychological interpretation,[23] could, in addition, be aligned with the way she is framed in doorways:

Elle se mettait à la fenêtre pour le voir partir; et elle restait accoudé sur le bord, entre deux pots de géraniums, vêtue de son peignoir, qui était lâche autour d'elle.   (I, p. 585)

Une jeune femme, en robe de mérinos bleu garnie de trois volants, vint sur le seuil de la maison.   (p. 579)[24]

Flaubert only once attempts to motivate his insistent use of window frames: 'elle s'y mettait souvent: la fenêtre, en province, remplace les théâtres et la promenade' (p. 617). Léon's departure from Yonville is framed in a window, as are the first appearance of Rodolphe, Emma's view of the *Comices* from the town hall, and a glimpse of Emma's child blowing a kiss as her mother rides off to the forest with Rodolphe. As Emma rides back again to Yonville: 'On la regardait des fenêtres' (p. 629). As in the eyes of the peasants in the garden of La Vaubyessard, Emma sees herself framed: her self-perception briefly coincides with the text's own representation of her.

Emma's set-piece view of Rouen is even described as having 'l'air immobile comme une peinture', and its framing is further emphasized by the fact that Emma views it through the carriage window (p. 663).[25] Barthes's well-known digression in *S/Z*, on 'le modèle de la peinture', perfectly illuminates this obsessive technique:

Toute description littéraire est une *vue*. On dirait que l'énonciateur, avant de décrire, se poste à la fenêtre, non tellement pour bien voir, mais pour fonder ce qu'il voit par son cadre même, l'embrasure fait le spectacle. Décrire, c'est donc placer le cadre vide que l'auteur réaliste transporte toujours avec lui (plus important que son chevalet), devant une collection ou un continu d'objets inaccessibles à la parole sans cette opération maniaque [...] pour pouvoir en parler, il faut que l'écrivain, par un rite initial, transforme d'abord le 'réel' en objet peint (encadré); après quoi il peut décrocher cet objet, le *tirer* de sa peinture; en un mot: le dé-peindre [...] Ainsi le réalisme (bien mal nommé, en tout cas souvent mal interprété) consiste, non à copier le réel, mais à copier une copie (peinte) du réel: ce fameux réel, comme sous l'effet d'une peur qui interdirait de le toucher directement, est *remis plus loin*, différé, ou du moins saisi à travers la gangue picturale dont on l'enduit avant de le soumettre à la parole.   (1970, p. 61)

Barthes suggests here that the framing of material is a half-way step to turning reality into literature. The many examples in Flaubert's works in which the 'real' is transformed into the 'imaginary' by the particular nature of characters' perceptions, can therefore be linked with Flaubert's own emphasis on the imaginary status of the reality represented in his novels.

The difficulty of sorting out the difference between the ontological status of a 'real' fictional character and that of an artistic representation of a character within that fiction, is underlined in the episode from *Madame Bovary* where Rodolphe finds Emma's painted miniature in his souvenir biscuit tin:

Il y avait auprès, se cognant à tous les angles, la miniature donnée par Emma; sa toilette lui parut prétentieuse et son regard en *coulisse* du plus pitoyable effet; puis, à force de considérer cette image et d'évoquer le souvenir du modèle, les traits d'Emma peu à peu se confondirent en sa mémoire, comme si la figure vivante et la figure peinte, se frottant l'une contre l'autre, se fussent réciproquement effacées. (I, p. 642)

This fusion, dissolving the difference between the Emma who was a flesh and blood mistress for Rodolphe, and her artistic representation as a miniature, has of course the effect of foregrounding her status as a represented character in Flaubert's novel. Here the interaction between literary representation and the illusion of reality created by that representation is played out in the story: the dialectic between Madame Bovary as character and *Madame Bovary* as novel is captured within Rodolphe's reverie.

Clearly, the status of 'reality' within Flaubert's fictions is related to, and should be evaluated through, the status of the fictions themselves. If Sartre is right that Flaubert would prefer to experience reality as if it were being imagined, Flaubert would indeed be attracted by the illusion of reality traditionally associated with representational art. The act of reading a 'classical' novel necessarily dissolves the distinction between the real and the imaginary. The neurotic's preferred manner of apprehending real experience — be he Flaubert or one of his characters — coincides with the reader's normal manner of processing the representation of fictional experience.

Conclusion
MAKING MADNESS MORE MAD

It is typical of Flaubert's general manner of representing 'real people' that references to the 'code of character' should ironically intensify, rather than undermine, the illusion of their reality. Consider the difference between the almost eighteenth-century aesthetic of self-consciousness followed in the 1845 *L'Éducation sentimentale*, and the heightening of the illusion of character in the final work, *Bouvard et Pécuchet*. In 1845 Flaubert pretends not to know everything about his characters: 'M. Dubois avait une redingote bleue, c'est tout ce que je peux en dire, ne l'ayant jamais vu que par derrière le dos' (I, p. 286); 'Mme Renaud a-t-elle eu un autre amant? c'est ce que j'ignore' (p. 371). He then inserts a final heavy-handed 'rangeons en rond tous les personnages au fond de la scène' (p. 371). In *Bouvard et Pécuchet*, the inclusion of the phrenology episode offers a fine illustration of his mature method. In a series of breathtaking successes in the art of 'cranioscopie', Bouvard and Pécuchet, turned amateur phrenologists, *accurately* read the characters of Victor and Victorine, Marcel, and most of the local villagers. As might be expected, Flaubert interpolates an argument with the local priest over the dangers of encouraging moral fatalism: 'Le voleur, l'assassin, l'adultère, n'ont plus qu'à rejeter leurs crimes sur la faute de leurs bosses' (II, p. 290). But this sort of humour takes second place to the climactic moment where the science of phrenology is used *to verify the characters of Bouvard and Pécuchet themselves*:

Mais avant d'instruire un enfant, il faudrait connaître ses aptitudes. On les devine par la phrénologie. Ils s'y plongèrent; puis voulurent en vérifier les assertions sur leurs personnes. Bouvard présentait la bosse de la bienveillance, de l'imagination, de la vénération et celle de l'énergie amoureuse: *vulgo* érotisme.

On sentait sur les temporaux de Pécuchet la philosophie et l'enthousiasme joints à l'esprit de ruse.

Effectivement, tels étaient leurs caractères. Ce qui les surprit, ce fut de reconnaître chez l'un comme chez l'autre le penchant à l'amitié, et, charmés de la découverte, ils s'embrassèrent avec attendrissement. (p. 290)

Making madness more mad

In a passage that may be thought to possess extraordinary relevance to Flaubert, Kierkegaard sets out what he means by the 'contemplative' aspect of irony:

> Were we to consider irony an inferior moment, we might allow it to be a sharp eye for what is crooked, wry, distorted, for what is erroneous, the vain in existence. In conceiving this it might seem that irony were identical with ridicule, satire, persiflage, etc. Naturally it has an affinity with this insofar as it, too, perceives what is vain, *but it differs in setting forth its observation*. It does not destroy vanity, it is not what punitive justice is in relation to vice, nor does it have the power of reconciliation within itself as does the comic. On the contrary, *it reinforces vanity in its vanity and renders madness more mad*. This is what might be called irony's attempt to mediate the discrete moments, not in a higher unity *but in a higher madness*.
>
> (1966, pp. 273–4, my emphases)

When Flaubert makes Bouvard and Pécuchet correctly discover their own characters in the phrenology episode, fictional madness is surely, and quite brilliantly, 'mediated in a higher madness'. Indeed Kierkegaard's description of the methods of irony is particularly appropriate to Flaubert's presentation of stupidity. His irony is never analytical, and deliberately magnifies rather than breaking down the madness at which it directs its entranced gaze.[1] Consider the joyful and *hurlant* meditation on the Plouharnel hat in *Par les Champs et par les grèves* — the hat is an ideally intractable aesthetic object in its unshatterable solidity — which is surely the prototype for Flaubert's 'setting forth of the observation' of irony in his major works:

> Qu'était-ce par devant? qui donc? le chapeau. Quel chapeau! un vaste et immense chapeau qui dépassait les épaules de son porteur et qui était en osier, quel osier! du bronze plutôt, planisphère dur et compact fait pour résister à la grêle, que la pluie ne traversait point, que le temps ne devait que durcir et fortifier. L'homme qu'il recouvrait disparaissait dessous et avait l'air d'y être entré jusqu'au milieu du corps, et il le portait cependant (je l'ai vu tourner la tête). Quelle constitution! quel tempérament il avait donc! quels muscles cervicaux! quelle force dans les vertèbres! Mais aussi quelle ampleur! quel cercle, ce chapeau! Il projette une ombre tout à l'entour de lui, et son maître ne doit jamais jouir du soleil. Ah! quel chapeau! c'est un couvercle de chaudière à vapeur surmonté d'une colonne, ça ferait un four en y pratiquent des meurtrières! Il y a des choses inébranlables: le Simplon et l'impudence des critiques, des choses solides: l'arc de l'Étoile et le français de Labruyère, des choses lourdes: le plomb, le bouilli de M. Nisard, des choses grandes: le nez de mon frère, l'*Hamlet* de Shakespeare et la tabatière de Bouilhet, mais je n'ai rien vu d'aussi solide, d'aussi inébranlable, d'aussi grand et aussi lourd que ce chapeau de Plouharnel.
>
> Et il avait une couverture en toile cirée! (II, p. 504)

The one-sentence paragraph with which this sustained piece of amazement so typically ends summarizes, increases and suspends the intensity of the effect of stupidity before the reader's eyes.[2]

Flaubert's characteristic and frequent use of exclamation marks is equally typical of his 'setting forth'. Crouzet, in his article on the 'epic style' of *Madame Bovary*, claims that the exclamation mark is the chief mechanism of a double admiration, a fusion of an inner and an outer viewpoint similar to that involved in Flaubert's use of *style indirect libre*. A sentence such as 'Mais ce qui attire le plus les yeux, c'est, en face de l'auberge du *Lion d'or*, la pharmacie de Monsieur Homais!' (I, p. 598) is an excellent example of a fusion of imbecility and esteem, an epic admiration which succeeds in capturing and fixing the stupidity (Crouzet, 1969, pp. 163–4). This 'fixing' is achieved, I would suggest, because at one level the exclamation marks are actually operated by the *reader*. Though remarks in *style indirect libre* are generally attributable to the 'voice' of a particular character or of the local community (and the first function of the exclamation mark is therefore the straightforward grammatical indication of a literal exclamation), the astonishment and delight are offered to the reader in all their opaque solidity:

Quelle joie, le lendemain en se réveillant! (II, p. 208)

Mais le plus beau, c'était, dans l'embrasure de la fenêtre, une statue de saint Pierre! (II, p. 233)

Ce qu'il y a d'important, c'est la philosophie de l'Histoire! (II, p. 240)

As the following random sample illustrates (a sample chosen from endless possibilities in all of the mature works), the modal effect of the reader's own amazed contemplation of characters' behaviour and reactions (encouraged by the exclamation mark), is to intensify the 'madness' and naivety rather than to destroy it or even to question it in any analytical way:

From *Madame Bovary*: Elle était morte! Quel étonnement! (I, p. 581); Mais Charles n'avait point d'ambition! (p. 595); C'est alors qu'Emma se repentit! (p. 633); Il fallut pourtant se séparer! (p. 661); Plus de doute, cette fois! (p. 691)

From *L'Éducation sentimentale*: Il avait donc trouvé sa vocation! (II, p. 26); Ruiné, dépouillé, perdu! (p. 41); Il héritait! [...] rien de plus vrai! toute la fortune de l'oncle! Vingt-sept mille livres de rente! (p. 43); Rien d'impossible maintenant! (p. 141); Et il devait être bien fort pour durer après une séparation si longue! (p. 161)

Making madness more mad

From *Un Cœur simple*: On le comparait à une dinde, à une b
de coups de poignard pour Félicité! Étrange obstination de Loul
plus du moment qu'on le regardait! (II, p. 174); et, quand ell
de perroquet! [...] Mais au haut de la côte, rien! [...] Loulo
avait-il fait? Peut-être qu'il s'était promené aux environs!

From *Bouvard et Pécuchet*: Alors Pécuchet fut libre! Avec quelle impatience
il attendait la sortie de Bouvard! Quel battement de cœur, dès que la porte
était refermée! (II, p. 260); Comment! la chair de Dieu se mêle à notre chair,
et elle n'y cause rien! (p. 281); Comment, pas de Grande Ourse! (p. 292)

I cannot, therefore, accept Jonathan Culler's influential claim that
irony is used to undermine representation.[3] It is true that Culler
speaks of the ironic withdrawal of Flaubert's novels when we try to
offer elaborate interpretations: '"What is all this fuss?" they might
say. "We are just novels: stories of Emma Bovary and Frédéric
Moreau, of Salammbô, Bouvard and Pécuchet, and Saint Antoine.
What has all this to do with us?"' (1974, p. 24). But Culler sees the
superficial appearance of an innocent story as a demoralizing trap:
having created a bond with the reader by the appearance of a readable
content, Flaubert breaks the contract by focusing attention on the
form, in order to devalue the content in which he does not believe.[4]

My own claim — that irony is at the heart of Flaubert's means of
representation — is an attempt to move beyond the false choice (story
or form) presented here by Culler, and to which I referred in my
introduction. The negative valuation currently attached to the notion
of a literary illusion takes the extreme form, in Ricardou, for example,
of scorn for anyone who might be 'taken in by it' rather than paying
proper attention to the work of the 'text'.[5] This is to ignore an
important theoretical need: that of taking account of what is precisely
the *illusion* that story precedes text. This is a problem that I believe
Barthes to have quietly solved through his theory of the workings of
myth, carefully explained in his analysis of the *Paris Match* cover of
a black soldier saluting the French flag.[6]

Barthes applies to myth — it is a short step to literature — his
favourite conceptual framework: the denotation/connotation grid
whereby the sign of the denotative system (relationship of signifier
and signified) becomes the signifier of a secondary 'hooked-on' sign
forming the connotative system. From one point of view it can be
shown that the denotation (saluting soldier 'captured' by the camera
as an innocent scene), acts as a prop for the more important secondary
connotation, its hidden ideological message that the French Empire is
a big happy family or whatever. But Barthes is also able to demonstrate

that the apparent logical priority of the denotation is actually a carefully mounted illusion on which the whole conjuring trick depends. If the *Paris Match* cover could always claim with a straight face to have no crafty political message at all, but to be quite simply a photograph of a Senegalese soldier saluting the French flag, this is because the pseudo-innocent air and sense of natural plenitude are established by what Barthes calls the 'turnstile' of form and meaning. Indeed myth's most valuable resource is the reader's unavoidable rotation through two alternating states:

> Mais le point capital en tout ceci, c'est que la forme ne supprime pas le sens, elle ne fait que l'appauvrir, l'éloigner, elle le tient à sa disposition. On croit que le sens va mourir, mais c'est une mort en sursis: le sens perd sa valeur, mais garde la vie, dont la forme du mythe va se nourrir. Le sens sera pour la forme comme une réserve instantanée d'histoire, comme une richesse soumise, qu'il est possible de rappeler et d'éloigner dans une alternance rapide: il faut sans cesse que la forme puisse reprendre racine dans le sens et s'y alimenter en nature; il faut surtout qu'elle puisse s'y cacher. (1957, p. 203)

With a simple but enormously persuasive argument, Barthes goes on to explain the *apparent* qualities of presence and plenitude of the content. Whereas Ricardou, analysing the literary text, declares the referential and the literal dimensions incompatible, and claims that the reader must either choose between the two or oscillate between them (1971, p. 36), for Barthes, *whichever term of the pair is concentrated upon, the other always plays a determining role*:

> Le mythe est une valeur, il n'a pas la vérité pour sanction: rien ne l'empêche d'être un alibi perpétuel: il lui suffit que son signifiant ait deux faces pour disposer toujours d'un ailleurs: le sens est toujours là pour *présenter* la forme; la forme est toujours là pour *distancer* le sens. Et il n'y a jamais contradiction, conflit, éclatement entre le sens et la forme: il ne se trouve jamais dans le même point. De la même façon, si je suis en auto et que je regarde le paysage à travers la vitre, je puis accommoder à volonté sur le paysage ou sur la vitre: tantôt je saisirai la présence de la vitre et la distance du paysage; tantôt au contraire la transparence de la vitre et la profondeur du paysage; mais le résultat de cette alternance sera constant: la vitre me sera à la fois présente et vide, le paysage me sera à la fois irréel et plein. (p. 209)

Barthes's spatial metaphor of the *alibi* conveys precisely the interaction of story and form: 'dans l'alibi aussi, il y a un lieu plein et un lieu vide, noués par un rapport d'identité négative ("je ne suis pas où vous croyez que je suis; je suis où vous croyez que je ne suis pas")' (p. 209). The permanently available alibi makes myth a slippery customer, and it is doubtless because literature is equally unanswerable to truth (whereas 'l'alibi ordinaire (policier, par exemple) a un ter... réel l'arrête, a un certain moment, de tourner' (p. 209)), that Barthe... analysis is so pertinent to the mechanics of literary representation.

Indeed Barthes includes in his theoretical essay on myth a brief but impressive discussion of *Bouvard et Pécuchet*. In Flaubert's novel he identifies yet another 'hooked-on' sign system, a second artificial myth produced by an overall ironic gaze at what he ventures to call the 'bouvard-et-pécuché-ité' celebrated in the story: 'Le pouvoir du second mythe, c'est de fonder le premier en naïveté regardée' (p. 223). It is precisely Flaubert's modal stance towards his subject matter that Barthes finds so important: 'les deux copieurs de codes scolaires sont eux-mêmes "représentés" dans un statut incertain, l'auteur n'usant d'aucun métalangage à leur égard (ou d'un métalangage en sursis)' (1970, p. 212). Flaubert is praised for thereby giving the problem of realism a solution which is 'franchement sémiologique' (1957, p. 223), by showing up its *method*. In this way Barthes manages to talk about Flaubert's 'realism' in a manner that avoids the pitfalls of treating it as the 'expression' or direct copying of the world, while his idea of the first system (the fiction), set up by the novel as a whole as an 'innocent' reality ('naïveté regardée'), is able to take account of the status and function of the illusion.

The same basic idea is picked up and generalized in *S/Z*, where Barthes argues that the interplay of the two reputedly different systems, denotation and connotation, serves the needs of the literary illusion:

> ce jeu assure avantageusement au texte classique une certaine *innocence*: des deux systèmes, dénotatif et connotatif, l'un se retourne et se marque: celui de la dénotation; la dénotation n'est pas le premier des sens mais elle feint de l'être [...] une phrase, quelque sens qu'elle libère, postérieurement, semble-t-il, à son énoncé, n'a-t-elle pas l'air de nous dire quelque chose de simple, de littéral, de primitif: de *vrai*, par rapport à quoi tout le reste (qui vient *après, au-dessus*) est littérature? (1970, p. 16)

Barthes's essential point is that denotation is not the first, literal meaning that it pretends to be, but, even in classical realism, the final and most important of connotations. If the literal message of the story seems a logically prior support for its literary elaboration and for the development of secondary, symbolic meanings, we have simply been duped. Doubtless in reading fiction we are willingly duped, for mental investment in the 'truth-value' of the illusion is the basic reading convention of representational novels.[7] The author's ploy is to foreground a false air of innocence in the denoted image, and to invite, with bare effrontery, a literal reading of the illusion of reality:

moments du texte, peut-être moins nombreux que vous
\, où la littéralité de l'énoncé − la dénotation − suffit
uiser son sens. Remarquons alors que, même à ce niveau,
ns connoté, qui est: *lisez-moi littéralement*.

(1981, p. 74)

˗supremely self-conscious representational writer, shows
˗˗˗ᴜ with serene confidence in the famous final summary of *La
Légende de Saint Julien l'Hospitalier*: 'Eh voila l'histoire de saint
Julien l'Hospitalier, telle à peu près qu'on la trouve, sur un vitrail
d'église, dans mon pays' (II, p. 187). The 'histoire' is the crowning
connotation from which the 'légende' pretends, paradoxically, to
originate. This device of a concluding summary is also found at the
end of *Salammbô* − 'Ainsi mourut la fille d'Hamilcar pour avoir
touché au manteau de Tanit' (I, p. 797) − where it sets a seal on the
'superstitious' reading of the events of the novel, as does the final
'shot' (enlargement?) of Félicité's simplicity: 'elle crut voir, dans les
cieux entr'ouverts, un perroquet gigantesque, planant au-dessus de
sa tête' (II, p. 177). These endings, like Flaubert's choice of ironic
clichés for his titles − *Mémoires d'un fou*, *L'Éducation sentimentale*
and *Un Cœur simple* − leave the reader with a very naive interpretation
of the illusion of reality represented in these works. A similar effect
is produced by simple titles based on the names of main characters
− *Madame Bovary*, *Salammbô* and *Bouvard et Pécuchet* − but
above all by Flaubert's pseudo-realist subtitles: 'Mœurs de Province'
and 'Histoire d'un jeune homme'. All invite the reader to share in
the narrator's own modal stance towards characters and events, a
stance of ingenuous affirmation that lends to the story the status of
a 'naïveté regardée'. '*Lisez-moi littéralement*': so speak the artless
summaries by which Flaubert, artfully *increasing* the power of the
naive illusion, closes off his texts and encloses their illusory characters.

NOTES

Introduction

1 Which leads to contradictions, as when F. R. Leavis denies implying that Flaubert is inferior to 'a George Moore', but cannot say why (1972, p. 18).

2 See especially Claudine Gothot-Mersch's study of *Madame Bovary* (1966) and her critical edition of *Bouvard et Pécuchet* (1979).

3 Martin Turnell's claim that *Madame Bovary* constitutes 'an onslaught on the whole basis of human feeling and on all spiritual and moral values' (1950, p. 264) develops to extremes the view put forward in Flaubert's day by Amélie Bosquet: 'Mais non! Ce n'est pas l'art, ce procédé sans sympathie et sans chaleur qui affaisse l'âme, qui tarit l'émotion, qui pétrifie à mesure qu'il crée, qui ne connaît ni l'enthousiasme ni la gaieté, qui ne sait pas renouveler la vie par un atome de vertu ou de bonheur, qui ne semble avoir d'autre but que d'exciter en nous un dégoût universel' (1965, p. 22).

4 Consider his own justification of a scene where Frédéric listens in great admiration to an elaborately described sample of Mme Arnoux's singing: 'Notez, pour me disculper, que mon héros n'est pas un musicien et que mon héroïne est une personne médiocre' (*Corr. Suppl.* IV, p. 278 (1879)). Clearly such characters are intended to be all that James thinks he has spotted.

5 As Jonathan Culler clearly explains: 'Stress on the interpersonal and conventional systems which traverse the individual, which make him a space in which forces and events meet rather than an individuated essence, leads to a rejection of a prevalent conception of character in the novel: that the most successful and "living" characters are richly delineated autonomous wholes, clearly distinguished from others by physical and psychological characteristics. This notion of character, structuralists would say, is a myth' (1975, p. 230).

6 A line pursued in Ann Jefferson's discussion of the poetics of character in the novel (1980, pp. 58–107).

7 Barthes's semic code in *S/Z* is a helpful way of reintroducing the study of psychological facets in a more properly semiotic fashion. The assumption that literary characters really are actual people would seem to lie behind Turnell's extraordinary claim that Flaubert 'hides' Emma's better

qualities: 'We cannot help noticing that Flaubert displayed a marked reluctance to give due weight to what was valid and genuine in Emma. She was not, as Henry James alleged, a woman who was "naturally depraved". She possessed a number of solid virtues which were deliberately played down by the novelist [...] We cannot withhold our approval from her attempts to improve her mind or from the pride that she took in her personal appearance and in the running of her house. The truth is that Flaubert sacrificed far too much to his *thèse*' (1950, p. 278).

8 D. Seed claims that 'James's concentration on character severely limits his reading of Flaubert' (1979, p. 316).

9 David Gervais, discussing James's reading of *Madame Bovary*, suggests that the division into two extreme responses (moral criticism balanced by exaggerated aesthetic praise and eulogy of form), might represent an attempted rationalization of a more divided overall response, a tugging of attraction and repulsion cutting across these avowed boundaries (1976, p. 25).

1. Oriental aesthetics

1 All page references to Flaubert's works (given after quotations in the text), are to: *Œuvres complètes*, edited by Bernard Masson, 2 vols. (Paris, Seuil (L'Intégrale), 1964).

2 To avoid confusion with references to other works by Sartre, page references to *L'Idiot de la famille*, 3 vols. (Paris, Gallimard, 1971−2), will be preceded by the abbreviation *L'Idiot* rather than by a date.

3 Where possible correspondence references are to Flaubert, *Correspondance*, edited by Jean Bruneau (Paris, Gallimard (Bibliothèque de la Pléiade), 1973−), abbreviated to *Corr.* (B). The two volumes published to date (1973 and 1980) cover the period to 1858. Later references are to Flaubert, *Correspondance*, 9 vols. (Paris, Conard, 1926−1933) and to *Correspondance. Supplément*, 4 vols. (Paris, Conard, 1954), abbreviated to *Corr.* (C) and *Corr. Suppl.* The year of the letter has been added in every case, but not the recipient.

4 'L'intuition artistique ressemble en effet aux hallucinations hypnagogiques − par son caractère de *fugacité*, − ça vous passe devant les yeux, − c'est alors qu'il faut se jeter dessus, avidement' (*Corr. Suppl.* II, p. 93 (1866)).

5 This is crucial of course to Sartre's life-long dilemma about the moral rightness of choosing the life of the imagination in a world in which children die of hunger. This certainly accounts to some extent for his love−hate relationship with Flaubert.

6 Thus, in *Questions de méthode*, praxis is defined as negativity in relation to the given situation, but positivity with respect to what is aimed at (1960, p. 129).

7 The whole section 'La Constitution' runs from p. 13 to p. 648. It is difficult to give precise references for any of the general summaries of Sartre's argument, partly because it tends to be rather repetitive.

8 The discussion of Octave Mannoni in the section entitled 'Le monde de l'envie' (*L'Idiot* I, pp. 422−52), examines in detail this idea of the 'fetishisation of the imaginary'. See Mannoni (1969, pp. 9−33) for the original account of the 'Je sais bien, mais quand même...' syndrome.

9 The best example is his play *Kean* (1954).

10 See too Sartre, 1940, pp. 242−3 for a brief discussion of the paradox of the actor.

11 The following have, however, taken all or part of Sartre's thesis seriously: Victor Brombert (1971), Jonathan Culler (1974), Naomi Schor (1976), Jeanne Bem (1975 and 1979), and Hazel Barnes (1981).

12 See also: 'Il me semble que je deviens bête comme un pot', and 'J'ai peut-être laissé mon intelligence là-bas' (*Corr.* (B) I, pp. 615 and 637 (1850)).

13 'Réflexion: les temples égyptiens m'embêtent profondément' (II, p. 581).

14 For Sartre's analysis of 'la Bêtise' see *L'Idiot* I, pp. 612−48. This is very well explained by Culler in his own analysis of the concept of stupidity in Flaubert (1974, pp. 157−84), though it will be seen that I disagree with his view of the function of stupidity in Flaubert's aesthetic. See, too, his slightly different conclusion to the problem in Laporte's recent collection of essays on *Bouvard et Pécuchet*, which is more in line with my own evaluation of the positive connection with reverie (1981, pp. 48−9).

15 'J'ai à faire une narration. Or le récit est une chose qui m'est très fastidieuse. Il faut que je mette mon héroïne dans un bal. Il y a si long-temps que je n'en ai vu un que ça me demande de grands efforts d'imagination' (*Corr.* (B) II, p. 83 (1852)).

16 'Il veut faire une féerie et avant de la faire, il lira toutes les féeries faites jusqu'à lui. Le singulier procédé d'imagination' (1956, I, p. 1024).

17 Albert Thibaudet appropriately describes *Salammbô* as 'une sorte d'astre mort comme la lune' (1935, p. 135), and suggests that Flaubert chose Carthage as an already opaque subject outside the mainstream of Western culture, so remote that even classical antiquity viewed it as: 'un bloc isolé, un aérolithe étranger par sa civilisation à ce qui l'entoure, un type de cité singulier qui a disparu, semble-t-il, sans laisser quoi que ce soit dans le cou-rant commun de la culture' (p. 131). Anne Green's recent book on *Salammbô* presents a vigorous argument against this view: 'It is certainly true that Flaubert delighted in history and derived enormous pleasure from reading accounts of life in the distant past; but to suggest that *Salammbô* is simply the indulgence of an escapist imagination is grossly to underestimate the significance of this complex novel' (1982, p. 58). Without wishing to devalue the many contemporary and universal parallels which she draws with the action and themes of the novel, there is surely much more at stake in the evacuation of present reality that Lukács, Brombert, Thibaudet and Sartre all attribute to Flaubert than a rather trivial escapist indulgence.

18 'Le palais s'éclaira d'un seul coup à sa plus haute terrasse, la porte du milieu s'ouvrit, et une femme, la fille d'Hamilcar elle-même, couverte de vêtements noirs, apparut sur le seuil' (I, p. 697); 'Mâtho, le portant ainsi, traversa toute la plaine jusqu'aux tentes des soldats, et le peuple, sur les murs, regardait s'en aller la fortune de Carthage' (p. 721); 'Autour du promontoire, comme le vent avait cessé, la voile tomba, et l'on aperçut auprès du pilote un homme debout, tête nue; c'était lui, le suffète Hamilcar!' (p. 728); 'Alors il se mit à courir sur la plate-forme d'un bout à l'autre, et comme un conducteur de char triomphant aux jeux Olympiques, Spendius, éperdu d'orgueil, levait les bras' (p. 769).

19 This is an almost exact reversal of Culler's analysis of *Salammbô*, part of his overall thesis that Flaubert's novels must be read as a challenge to the easy construction of meaning, that in demoralizing his readers by making them read his works as autonomous verbal objects, he will eventually lead them to try to fill this 'absence' with a 'fully self-conscious understanding': 'in place of the novel as mimesis we have the novel as structure playing with different modes of ordering, and enabling the reader to understand how he makes sense of the world' (1975, p. 238). *Salammbô* is seen as a perfect allegory for the formal desire for connection and meaning, since its characters, Culler claims, are engaged in a desperate attempt to understand their relationship to their situation, recognizing strangeness but trying to overcome it. Their bewilderment is a metaphor for that of the reader: 'the rebuffs they encounter or solutions they discover offer an explicit thematization of the problems of reading' (1974, p. 212). For all readers, Culler would claim, difference and strangeness are a gap to be bridged by self-conscious interpretation: 'the strange, the formal, the fictional, must be recuperated or naturalized, brought within our ken, if we do not want to remain gaping before monumental inscriptions' (1975, p. 134). Not only does the attribution of such didactic aims to *Flaubert* seem inappropriate, but to leave his readers 'gaping before monumental inscriptions' would certainly have been his idea of perfect success. My own argument has been to link Flaubert's aesthetic of reading to the more or less deliberate refusal of characters to understand the world and to interpret their situation.

2. The merits of inarticulacy

1 Especially in the early works, and normally in the context of artistic creation: 'Comment rendre par des mots ces choses pour lesquelles il n'y a pas de langage?' (I, p. 238); 'Pouvez-vous dire par des mots le battement du cœur?' (p. 247). Such remarks can be classified of course under the familiar Romantic cliché of the incommensurability of language and experience; however, Flaubert's insistence upon this theme far outlives his imitations of Romantic literature.

2 'il faut que mon bonhomme [...] vous émeuve pour tous les veufs' (*Corr.* (B) II, p. 346 (1853)).

3   For example on the return journey from La Vaubyessard (Pommier and Leleu, 1949, pp. 218–19).

4   'cette faculté de s'assimiler à toutes les misères et de se supposer les ayant est peut-être la vraie charité humaine. Se faire ainsi le centre de l'humanité, tâcher enfin d'être son cœur général où toutes les veines éparses se réunissent, ... ce serait à la fois l'effort du plus grand et du meilleur homme?' (*Corr.* (B) II, p. 346 (1853)).

5   As for Charles, much of Justin's direct speech is removed from the drafts, for example the discussion about the tilbury and groom (Pommier and Leleu, 1949, p. 536).

6   In a draft Dussardier is described as follows: 'Ce gros garçon avait l'âme plus délicate qu'une marquise. Avec ses fortes épaules & ses bons yeux, il rappelait les forgerons que l'on voit au bord des routes, tenant sur leurs bras un petit enfant [...] Quoiqu'il n'eut pas d'esprit Fred. goûtait dans sa compagnie un certain charme' (B.N. n.a.fr. 17605, fol. 167ʳ).

7   Discussing this Culler claims: 'We are amused, no doubt, but we do not want to class ourselves with Bourais by joining in his amusement. We prefer to be won over by her innocence and unpretentiousness, valuing the sense of our own broadmindedness that comes from protecting or defending one so charmingly vulnerable' (1974, p. 209). Doubtless my view of inarticulacy leaves me open to the dreadful charge of 'protecting the charmingly vulnerable', and I can only rely on the reader's good will to protect my own vulnerability on this issue.

8   Whereas when she takes communion herself the next day the experience is less real: 'Elle la reçut dévotement, mais n'y goûta pas les mêmes délices' (p. 170).

3. By-passing speech

1   Sartre claims that because Flaubert is deprived of a sense of both his own reality and external reality, he fails to master the affirmative use of language. As a passive child with nothing to communicate, he never understands the function of speech. He tends to believe that language is something already there, coming to him from outside, and belonging to other people rather than serving as an instrument of his own attempt at self-expression, at establishing a relationship between himself and the world. He learns to decode verbal messages without properly connecting words with everyday life, still seeing them from the outside, as things, even when he produces them himself.

2   Genette claims that 'difficulté' is the final level of form distinguishing Flaubert's mature works from the early ones and from his letters, and the finished pages from the rough drafts. While Valéry treats Flaubert's obsession with 'l'accessoire' as a fault (1960, I, p. 618), for Genette the passion for insignificant details is central to his writing. Unlike Balzac's descriptive details which normally have an explanatory or metaphorical

function, Flaubert's are strategically placed to distract the reader from the activity of investing meaning in the story (1966 (b), p. 239). This radical device contests the normal demands of the novel as genre: 'Interposant cette *lourde porte opaque*, ces *ombres du soir*, cette *petite lyre d'ébène* entre un réseau de signes et un univers de sens, il défait un langage et instaure un silence' (1963, p. 57). He regards Flaubert as someone who had plenty to say (he attributes to the early works and the letters a verbal facility packed with meaning), but who at some point decides, 'comme par surcroît', to say nothing. The correspondence is full of the aesthetic aspect of writing (full of his desire for perfection, for example), but passes over its semantic aspect: the 'désamorçage' of expression, the transformation of the signifying discourse into an opaque and somehow silent object. Flaubert's particular use of language 'paralysed' the subject matter of his novels into a sort of silence, and Genette describes the 'death of language' (its loss of meaning) as 'un peu *aussi* le travail de Flaubert' (p. 57).

3   Though in different contexts language acquires leaden and potentially sinister qualities. Consider the counterpointing of Charles's untimely exclamation, 'C'était peut-être un valgus', with the screams of the newly amputated Hippolyte: 'Au choc imprévu de cette phrase tombant sur sa pensée comme une balle de plomb dans un plat d'argent, Emma tressaillant leva la tête pour deviner ce qu'il voulait dire' (I, p. 637), or the macabre mercenary invention for the siege of Carthage: 'Ces atroces projectiles portaient des lettres gravées qui s'imprimaient dans les chairs; et, sur les cadavres, on lisait des injures, telles que *pourceau, chacal, vermine*, et parfois des plaisanteries: *attrape!* ou *je l'ai bien mérité*' (I, p. 773).

4   See Gothot-Mersch's critical edition of the novel (1979) and Mouchard and Neefs's 'Vers le second volume: *Bouvard et Pécuchet*' (1980) for recent discussions of the problems associated with the second volume.

5   See too his occasional likening of the process of writing to masturbation: 'd'aller vivre avec toi, en toi, et de reposer ma tête entre tes seins au lieu de me la masturber sans cesse, pour en faire éjaculer des phrases' (*Corr.* (B) II, p. 459 (1853)); 'Enfin l'érection est arrivée, monsieur, à force de me fouetter et de me manustirper. Espérons qu'il y aura fête' (*Corr.* (B) II, p. 845 (1858)).

6   Sartre claims that one of Flaubert's most basic intentions as a stylist is to find an equivalent of oral seduction. This is part of a suggestive discussion of Flaubert's relationship with his voice (*L'Idiot* I, pp. 876–88), the vehicle of his verbal malaise in that it seems both to escape him and to give him away. Sartre supposes that acting was seen as an opportunity to reappropriate his being by fascinating others with his voice (note Bouvard and Pécuchet's voice-training sessions). When this vocation is frustrated and he passes to writing he remains forever alienated from his voice. Sartre proposes viewing Flaubert's whole creative project in terms of a relationship with his voice, from the rhetoric of the early works,

to the 'causons un peu' of his letters (where meaning seems a marginal intention), to the 'refused eloquence' of the mature works, where the sheer physicality of words founds the attempted seduction of the reader. The basic idea is taken from Thibaudet: 'Flaubert, dont la nature est essentiellement oratoire, et que toutes ses œuvres de jeunesse nous manifestent comme un talent oratoire, l'élimine de plus en plus à partir de *Madame Bovary*' (1935, p. 226); 'Il est le seul des prosateurs du XIXe siècle dont le style ait eu besoin de ce contact dernier avec la parole, avec les timbres de la voix et le rhythme de la respiration. C'est que, comme nous l'avons vu, le fond de ce style est oratoire, se définit comme l'oratoire qui, à partir de *Madame Bovary*, se dépouille, est mis au point, se résout en dissonances pour se reformer en consonances' (pp. 278–9).

4. Endless illusions

1 Prendergast, alluding to Homais's famous mirror scene omitted from the final version of *Madame Bovary* (Pommier and Leleu, 1949, p. 129), characterizes Flaubert's novel as a 'play of mirrors', as opposed to the fixed mirror often associated with the classical realist novel (1975, pp. 212–13).

2 In other words Poulet reduces questions of chronology to the nature of Flaubert's perception, assuming that the only artistic problem is to subsequently convey this intimation: 'Dès lors le problème du temps n'est plus qu'un problème du style' (1950, p. 326).

3 Also: 'Et il se mit à l'aimer, à aimer sa main, ses gants, ses yeux, même quand ils regardaient un autre, sa voix quand elle lui disait bonjour, les robes qu'elle portait, mais surtout ce qu'elle avait le matin, une façon de sarrau rose à larges manches et sans ceinture, à aimer la chaise où elle s'asseyait, tous les meubles de sa chambre, la maison entière, la rue où était cette maison' (I, p. 292).

4 See Gleize (1974) for an impressive analysis of plot repetitions in *L'Éducation sentimentale*.

5 Note that by using pomade on his moustache he is imitating both the Vicomte at La Vaubyessard and Rodolphe, and thereby completes and recalls that particular chain of references.

6 I could not therefore agree with Ross Chambers's recent reading of *Un Cœur simple* which, despite a sophisticated overall argument, appears to give a negative evaluation of this very aspect of Félicité: 'dans la mesure où il s'agit d'un culte de l'objet *matériel*, et non de l'objet pris comme "signifiant" – Félicité montrera le côté négatif de sa "simplicité", aspect déplaisant de sa spontanéité affective faisant contraste sur le plan esthétique avec ce côté positif de la même spontanéité qu'est sa capacité imaginative' (1981, p. 786).

7 See Thorlby (1956): 'The resolution of such suffering and love as Félicité's is made in heaven, and across the very threshold Flaubert draws his most

daring line. / In retrospect the whole story appears built to support it' (pp. 58—9). However, Thorlby is making a different point from my own. The irony of the ending of *Un Cœur simple* will be placed in a different perspective in my conclusion.

8 See Raymonde Debray-Genette's analysis of the ubiquity of metonymic processes (1970).

9 While a statue portrays 'saint Michel terrassant le dragon' (p. 169), perhaps an ironic reference to Félicité's encounter with the bull.

10 Shoshana Felman (1974) details all sorts of repetitions of this kind. However she adopts an ideological perspective on repetition which is different from my own.

11 Genette accounts for the peculiarities of what he christens the 'pseudo-itératif' by a sort of conventional artistic licence, into the spirit of which the reader can easily enter: 'une scène singulière a été comme arbitraire-ment, et sans aucune modification si ce n'est dans l'emploi des temps, convertie en scène itérative [...] bref, le pseudo-itératif constitue typique-ment dans le récit classique une *figure* de rhétorique narrative, qui n'exige pas d'être prise à la lettre, bien au contraire: le récit affirment littéralement "ceci se passait tous les jours" pour faire entendre figurément: "tous les jours il se passait quelque chose de ce genre, dont ceci est une réalisation parmi d'autres"' (1972, p. 152).

12 In what seems to me basically an unusual gloss on the well-known theme of Emma refinding in adultery the platitudes of marriage, word-play ('tour' and 'trou', 'nouer' and 'Rouen') becomes symptomatic of a crisis in language, a loss of difference which parallels society's inability to main-tain differences and distinctions and 'the realm where adulterous relation-ships obtain' (1979, p. 365): 'all these apparent opposites and many others gradually, or rapidly, lose their differential features. The triumph of adultery is the destruction of difference' (p. 367).

13 Nathalie Sarraute, referring to the sunrise in *Salammbô*, calls the phrase 'çà et là' precisely a 'brief quiver' (1966, p. 197). See too Pierre Danger: 'Pour concilier la précision du détail et l'amplitude qu'il veut conserver à certaines scènes, Flaubert use fréquemment d'un procédé très simple: l'ex-pression "çà et là" qui permet de fixer un détail en le multipliant en quelque sorte à l'infini pour retrouver l'espace nécessaire' (1973, pp. 215—16).

14 Repeated readings of the story would turn even singular events into iterated ones. Roger Huss (1977, p. 145) suggests the possibility of inter-ference between the iterative imperfect and the grammatically anomalous imperfect (replacing the more normal past historic), which is the subject of his analysis: that the reader, influenced by the specificity of events presented as repeated ones, might disregard the information in temporal adverbs like 'souvent', reinterpret events as singular, and accommodate the imperfect by reading it as an anomalous one. I would suggest that this interference might equally work in the opposite direction: that the anomalous imperfect might be sensed as an iterative one.

15 'Je maintiens qu'une œuvre d'art (digne de ce nom et faite avec conscience) et inappréciable, n'a pas de valeur commerciale, ne peut pas se payer' (*Corr.* (C) VI, p. 458 (1872)). See too Barthes (1970, pp. 22–3): 'La relecture, opération contraire aux habitudes commerciales et idéologiques de notre société qui recommande de "jeter" l'histoire une fois qu'elle a été consommée ("dévorée"), pour que l'on puisse alors passer à une autre histoire, acheter un autre livre, et qui n'est tolérée que chez certaines catégories marginales de lecteurs (les enfants, les vieillards et les professeurs), la relecture est ici proposée d'emblée, car elle seule sauve le texte de la répétition (ceux qui négligent de relire s'oblige à lire partout la même histoire), le multiplie dans son divers et son pluriel: elle le tire hors de la chronologie interne ("ceci se passe *avant* ou *après* cela") et retrouve un temps mythique (sans *avant* ni *après*).'

16 The deformations of syntax, the unusual use of tense, conjunctions, prepositions and adjectives that Proust (1927) and Thibaudet (1935) describe so well. These once caused Leo Bersani to conclude that the 'high priest of style is thus the master of the rhythmical tic' (1968, p. 66), and Michel Picard to claim that 'la magie du style flaubertien' is essentially a source of esoteric pleasure for a few well-practised ears (1973, p. 79).

17 If, as Genette suggests (1966(a), pp. 155–6), once language simply imitates itself it has moved out of the realm of *mimesis* altogether: 'Nous sommes donc conduits à cette conclusion inattendue, que le seul mode que connaisse la littérature en tant que représentation est le récit, équivalent verbal d'événements non verbaux et aussi [...] d'événements verbaux, sauf à s'effacer dans ce dernier cas devant une citation directe où s'abolit toute fonction représentative, à peu près comme un orateur judiciaire peut interrompre son discours pour laisser le tribunal examiner lui-même une pièce à conviction. La représentation littéraire, la *mimesis* des anciens, ce n'est donc pas le récit plus les "discours": c'est le récit, et seulement le récit. Platon opposait *mimesis* à *diegesis* comme une imitation parfaite à une imitation imparfaite; mais l'imitation parfaite n'est plus une imitation, c'est la chose même, et finalement la seule imitation, c'est l'imparfaite. *Mimesis*, c'est *diegesis*.'

18 'Thibaudet avait remarqué qu'il existe souvent dans la production des très grands écrivains, une *œuvre-limite*, une œuvre singulière, presque gênante, dans laquelle ils déposent à la fois le secret et la caricature de leur création, tout en y suggérant l'œuvre aberrante qu'ils n'ont pas écrite et qu'ils auraient peut-être voulu écrire: cette sorte de rêve où se mêlent d'une façon rare le positif et le négatif d'un créateur, c'est la *Vie de Rancé* de Chateaubriand, c'est le *Bouvard et Pécuchet* de Flaubert' (Barthes, 1964, p. 80); 'Une existence littéraire, depuis Rousseau, se conclut volontiers sur ces œuvres qui scandalisent le conformisme de la critique, mais où un artiste, à l'heure de la vieillesse et de la mort, a au moins la satisfaction d'ouvrir toute son arrière-boutique, et de parler net, avant de partir' (Thibaudet, 1935, pp. 219–20).

19 'Les livres ne se font pas comme les enfants, mais comme les pyramides, avec un dessin prémédité, et en apportant des grands blocs l'un par-dessus l'autre, à force des reins, de temps et de sueur, et ça ne sert à rien! et ça reste dans le désert! mais en le dominant prodigieusement' (*Corr.* (B) II, p. 783 (1857)).

20 For a very interesting discussion of the history of the animals/parents ambiguity in the drafts, see De Biasi (1980, pp. 78–88).

21 In a way reminiscent of the dispersion of the fire *mise en abyme* in Butor's *L'Emploi du temps* – see Ricardou, 1967, pp. 185–8.

22 'Elle les coucha elle-même dans son lit, puis ferma la croisée; ils s'endormirent' (p. 185); 'Les vitraux garnis de plomb obscurcissaient la pâleur de l'aube [...] il avançait vers le lit, perdu dans les ténèbres au fond de la chambre' (p. 185). The window also acts as a frame for Julien's abortive hunting expedition, especially given the reference to the singing birds: 'et, derrière le vitrail, les petits oiseaux commençaient à chanter' (p. 185).

23 J. O'Connor views the leper in a similar way: 'There is some case for doubt, therefore, whether Julien "really" meets a leper – or Christ – at the end or whether this figure may not equally well be interpreted as representing emblems of aspects of himself' (1980, p. 821).

5. Overturning reality

1 Sartre himself is loath to evaluate a neurosis by any 'objective' notion of what constitutes a normal or an abnormal attitude. Hence his sympathy for the approach of R. D. Laing: 'Je pense comme vous qu'on ne peut comprendre les troubles psychiques *du dehors*, à partir du déterminisme positiviste ni les reconstruire par une combinaison de concepts qui restent extérieures à la maladie vécue' (Sartre's 1963 preface to Laing and Cooper's *Reason and Violence*, 1971, p. 7).

2 Many critics have taken Jules as a *permanent* mouthpiece for Flaubert's mature aesthetic, for example Bruneau: 'Flaubert conservera toujours les idées philosophiques de Jules, il ne changera rien non plus à son esthétique' (1962, p. 465). But Flaubert merely uses him to define an abstract artistic stance, and his aesthetic only really embodies a set of rules of conduct for the artist, and an attitude to the world without which he cannot even proceed with his task (pantheism, universal sympathy, impersonality and irony). These generalizations reveal very little about the sort of novels that Flaubert will go on to write, indeed the discussion of Jules's art does not even mention novels, for after his play it is not at all clear what he is supposed to have written. All we learn is that at one stage he is writing a history of Asian migrations and composing a volume of poetry at the same time, and note that he actually has quite contradictory aesthetic aims for each: the former is to be dominated by 'une unité puissante et réelle', but for the latter 'il travaillait à assouplir le rythme à tous les caprices de la pensée, c'était une couleur en relief, avec des fantaisies saisissantes, une musique ailée' (I, p. 327).

3 'le corps fatigué, l'œil morne et béant' (I, p. 212); 'Antoine, immobile, reste les yeux fixés sur l'horizon, la bouche béante et les bras levés' (I, p. 465).

4 Compare Frédéric and Rosanette's experience on the way back from the races: 'et les figures se succédaient avec une vitesse d'ombres chinoises. Frédéric et Rosanette ne se parlaient pas, éprouvant une sorte d'hébétude à voir auprès d'eux continuellement toutes ses roues tourner' (II, p. 84).

5 'Quelque temps encore je restai, béant, à savourer le battement de mon cœur et le dernier tressaillement de mes nerfs agités' (I, p. 260); 'elle se rapprocha de moi avec étonnement et, me prenant par le bras, comme si j'étais une illusion qu'elle voulait saisir' (p. 262).

6 See also: 'Et il en restait là, béant et affamé devant ce mets qui fumait pour lui seul' (I, p. 296).

7 Likening Sherrington to Mr Gradgrind in Dickens's *Hard Times*, Culler convincingly dismisses his view of Flaubert's intention in *Salammbô*: 'one might well wonder why he should have bothered to resuscitate Carthage if it was only to show that Carthaginians were prey to religious delusion and refused to face facts' (1974, p. 217).

8 See Jean-Pierre Richard's remarks on the difference between Frédéric's and Emma's attitude to reality (1970, pp. 224–5): 'Emma Bovary, elle aussi, refusait le réel; mais elle était trop profondément attirée par lui pour vivre en pure gratuité dans le monde de son imagination. Elle tâchait alors de faire coexister la rêverie romanesque avec la satisfaction charnelle, gâchant le plus souvent l'une par l'autre, et perdant finalement sur tous les plans.'

9 See Picard (1973).

10 'He organizes into compact and unequivocal discourse the confused impressions of discomfort which arise in Emma at sight of the room, the meal, her husband' (p. 488). He is analysing the passage: 'Mais c'était surtout aux heures de repas qu'elle n'en pouvait plus, dans cette petite salle au rez-de-chaussée, avec le poêle qui fumait, la porte qui criait, les murs qui suintaient, les pavés humides; toute l'amertume de l'existence lui semblait servie sur son assiette, et, à la fumée du bouilli, il montait du fond de son âme comme d'autres bouffées d'affadissement. Charles était long à manger; elle grignotait quelques noisettes, ou bien, appuyée du coude, s'amusait, avec la pointe de son couteau, à faire des raies sur la toile cirée' (I, p. 596).

11 '"Mais non, je vous jure!" et du bras gauche il lui entoura la taille; ils se ralentirent. Le vent était mou, les étoiles brillaient, l'énorme charretée de foin oscillait devant eux; et les quatre chevaux, en traînant leurs pas, soulevaient de la poussière. Puis, sans commandement, ils tournèrent à droite. Il l'embrassa encore une fois. Elle disparut dans l'ombre' (*Un Cœur simple*, II, p. 167).

12 Leo Bersani (1974) points out that Flaubert finds life so little worth bothering about that the superficial argument for literature's violation

113

of experience has little force. Flaubert cares more about the violation of literature, and indirectly criticizes Emma's expectations as a reader. For Emma tells Léon that she finds poetry boring, she only enjoys stories of non-stop action 'où l'on a peur' (I, p. 602). Her need to get some sort of personal profit even from her reading is amusingly described by Bersani as a parody of all claims for the relevance of art to life. In encouraging readers to search in life for the abstractions invented in books, the moral tradition could be accused of contributing to the sins of inferior literary romance, the realistic claims of which depend upon ignoring their own mediating processes, ignoring the *work* of the writer. Flaubert's writing is viewed as a continuous correction, through stylistic example, of Emma's confusions, for it constantly draws attention to its own nature as a composed written document: 'the Flaubertian workshop is one in which a master craftsman − somewhat at the expense of his own craft − teaches us to read' (p. 28). In other words Bersani sees Emma as providing an object lesson in 'how not to read literature'.

13 See Culler's analysis of her desire to 'devenir une sainte' (1974, pp. 188−9).

14 See too the first *Éducation*: 'Quand ils étaient séparés, quand ils étaient loin l'un de l'autre, leur image réciproque s'offrait à leur esprit, rayonnante d'excitations irrésistibles; mais lorsqu'ils se retrouvaient, un étonnement subit leur arrivait au cœur à se revoir, simples comme par le passé et déjà mille fois connus. Ces sortes de désillusions inavouées se tournaient en désirs nouveaux' (I, p. 330).

15 Percy Lubbock contends that there is not enough in Emma to make her the main character in a drama, and that all the interest lies in the way Flaubert presents a simple case, that while the 'fact' of Emma is entirely serious her value is quite a different matter, that Flaubert always knows her to be worthless (1926, p. 89).

16 Bibliothèque historique de la ville de Paris, MS Flaubert, carnet 19, folio 25.

17 The superiority of imagination and memory over actual experience has its first important exploration in *Mémoires d'un fou*: 'Comment aurait-elle pu en effet voir que je l'aimais, car je ne l'aimais pas alors, et en tout ce que je vous ai dit, j'ai menti; c'était maintenant que je l'aimais, que je la désirais; que, seul sur le rivage, dans les bois ou dans les champs, je me la créais là, marchant à côté de moi; me parlant, me regardant [...] je crus entendre Maria marcher près de moi; elle me tenait par le bras et tournait la tête pour me voir, c'était elle qui marchait dans les herbes. Je savais bien que c'était une hallucination que j'animais moi-même, mais je ne pouvais me défendre d'en sourire et je me sentais heureux' (I, p. 246).

18 See Neefs, 1981, pp. 117−18, for a discussion of this passage.

19 Barthes alludes here to Lacan's notion of *l'Imaginaire*, but it seems likely that he is also influenced by the very different early writings of Sartre. His

final work, *La Chambre claire* (1980) bears the dedication: 'En hommage à *L'Imaginaire* de Sartre'.

20 Victor Brombert (1975, p. 74), suggesting that there is a way of envisaging life in the future anterior, is surely looking for a term like the aesthetic attitude: 'Mais si j'ai insisté sur le futur antérieur dans *L'Éducation*, ce n'est pas que cette phrase-là me paraisse une clé unique, c'est qu'il correspond à un mode, à une perspective, et qu'il est en soi une métaphore. Il y a une façon d'envisager la vie au futur antérieur sans même qu'il y ait nécessairement futur antérieur grammatical.' It is because Mme Arnoux and Frédéric *always* take the aesthetic attitude to their relationship, that I cannot agree with Jonathan Culler that the way they turn their 'affair' into a great literary event is 'an arbitrary conferral of meaning' on the past (1974, p. 154).

21 In a draft (n.a.fr. 17610, fol. 65^r), when Frédéric asks why she had hidden, Mme Arnoux replies 'Vous ne le devinez pas?', and Flaubert inserts in brackets: 'ce qui voulait dire j'avais peur de baiser avec vous'.

22 'Jamais elle ne lui avait paru si captivante, si profondément belle. De temps à autre, une aspiration soulevait sa poitrine; ses deux yeux fixes semblaient dilatés par une vision intérieure, et sa bouche demeurait entreclose comme pour donner son âme. Quelquefois, elle appuyait dessus fortement son mouchoir; il aurait voulu ce petit morceau de batiste tout trempé de larmes. Malgré lui, il regardait la couche, au fond de l'alcôve, en imaginant sa tête sur l'oreiller; et il voyait cela si bien, qu'il se retenait pour ne pas la saisir dans ses bras. Elle ferma les paupières, apaisée, inerte. Alors il s'approcha de plus près, et, penché sur elle, il examinait avidement sa figure. Un bruit de bottes résonna dans le couloir, c'était l'autre. Ils l'entendirent fermer la porte de sa chambre. Frédéric demanda, d'un signe, à Mme Arnoux, s'il devait y aller.

Elle répliqua "oui" de la même façon; et ce muet échange de leurs pensées était comme un consentement, un début d'adultère' (II, p. 69). In a scenario (n.a.fr. 17611, fol. 24^r), Flaubert notes (crossed out): 'Le lecteur doit croire qu'il va baiser Mme Arnoux.' But the passage quoted from the final version merely connotes a physical communion and I doubt if the frequenter of Flaubert would expect it to take place in reality.

23 Notably by Rousset: 'La fenêtre est un poste privilégié pour ces personnages flaubertiens à la fois immobiles et portés à la dérive, englués dans leur inertie et livrés au vagabondage de leur pensée; dans le lieu fermé où l'âme moisit, voilà une déchirure par où se diffuser dans l'espace sans avoir à quitter son point de fixation' (1962, p. 123).

24 Compare the first view of Salammbô: 'Le palais s'éclaira d'un seul coup à sa plus haute terrasse, la porte du milieu s'ouvrit, et une femme, la fille d'Hamilcar elle-même, couverte de vêtements noirs, apparut sur le seuil' (I, p. 697).

25 There are many framed views in the travel notes, e.g.: 'Paysage grandiose et dur, encadré (lorsqu'on arrive) par deux vieux gazis' (II, p. 578);

'Effet du soleil vu par la porte du grand temple à demi comblé par le sable; c'est comme par un soupirail' (p. 581); 'Rien n'est joli comme la campagne vue dans l'encadrement d'une arche d'un de ces ponts ou d'un aqueduc, surtout quand passent dessous des chameaux ou des mulets' (p. 604).

Conclusion

1 Flaubert's handling of stereotypes is therefore far removed from the skilful pinpointing and dismantling of petit-bourgeois rhetoric of a Roland Barthes, and I cannot therefore accept Christopher Prendergast's promotion of Flaubert as an admirable example of the '*undoing* of the stereotype': 'what the text operates is a subversion of *fixity*, a negation of fixed, absolute or, better, *stereotyped* definitions of reality. What fascinates Flaubert, what animates and nourishes the negative impetus in his imagination, is the figure of the *Stereotype*, those diverse forms of attitude, behaviour, language, all the activity of which is to transform provisional constructs of reality into stereotyped certitudes of absolute Truth. In this sense, it is preferable to speak of the Flaubert text not as "destructive" (in the sense of some blind nihilistic rage), but, adopting a term from Jacques Derrida, as "de-constructive", as systematically deconstructing all those particular constructions of reality that are hypostasized, uncritically and complacently, as the Real *tout court*, the Real in some absolute, fixed sense' (1975, pp. 203—4). Barthes himself, in a passage undeniably Flaubertian in inspiration, deliberately renounces his own analytical talents to celebrate an aesthetic fascination with stupidity which precisely captures the flavour of Flaubert's near hysterical delight in things foolish: 'D'un jeu musical entendu chaque semaine à F.M. et qui lui paraît "bête", il tire ceci: la bêtise serait un noyau dur et insécable, un *primitif*: rien à faire pour la décomposer *scientifiquement* (si une analyse scientifique de la bêtise était possible, toute la TV s'effondrerait). Qu'est-elle? Un spectacle, une fiction esthétique, peut-être un fantasme? Peut-être avons-nous envie de nous mettre dans le tableau? C'est beau, c'est suffocant, c'est étrange,. et de la bêtise je n'aurai le droit de dire, en somme, que ceci: qu'*elle me fascine*. La fascination, ce serait le sentiment *juste* que doit m'inspirer la bêtise (si on en vient à prononcer le nom): elle m'étreint (elle est intraitable, rien n'a barre sur elle, elle vous prend dans le jeu de la main chaude)' (1975, pp. 55—6).
2 See too 'Et elle avait la crotte aux yeux!' (II, p. 525), which completes a sustained description of a woman in the same work. Debray-Genette's analysis of the description of the inn room at Carnac (II, p. 493) concludes: 'Flaubert, dans cette œuvre, n'a certes pas encore perdu l'habitude des commentaires et des comparaisons qui relèvent du discours du narrateur. Le progrès à venir sera de faire rendre l'âme à une casquette, à une pièce montée, à une pharmacie, sans aucun commentaire. Le trait

final, minuscule, suffira à faire basculer dans le grotesque' (1982, p. 154). However the 'trait final' seems already perfected in the Plouharnel hat.

3   Nevertheless Culler has provided an adventurous discussion of Flaubert's irony, which forms the turning point of his whole 'uses of uncertainty' argument (1974, pp. 185–207). Irony is seen as another mechanism for blocking normal and easy ways of reading Flaubert's novels, for setting up an empty or 'uncertain' space, of which the reader can only make sense by passing to the formal organizing category that Culler calls 'the sacred', where understanding is secure because fully self-conscious. The corrosive irony therefore destroys in the cause of an ultimately more correct interpretation. Though Culler's attempt to replace a mimetic view of the novels with a semiotic one is rigorously and inventively pursued, the attempt to attribute almost didactic motives to Flaubert's irony (aiming at the reader's increased awareness of man as *homo significans*), runs totally counter to my own view of Flaubert's aesthetic aims.

4   Prendergast struggles very intelligently with the implications of this view, to arrive at a suggestion with which I agree: 'one can equally argue that the story does not remain readable (i.e. representational) as a ruse designed to throw into sharper relief the ironic "deconstruction" of the conventions of narrative presentation; that it does not masquerade as a Novel in order to operate obliquely as an "anti-Novel". Rather, if the story remains readable, this would simply be because, at one level, it *is* readable, profoundly complicit in the classic discourse of representation' (1981, pp. 270–1). However I am sure that Prendergast is wrong to attribute Culler's view ('movement from the surface appearance of innocence to the deeper recognition of irony') to *Barthes*, whose various discussions (of which I quote several in the course of this chapter), appear to support and go beyond Prendergast's own claims. When Barthes speaks of Flaubert as maintaining 'un état très subtil, presque intenable, du discours: la narrativité est déconstruite *et l'histoire reste cependant lisible*' (1973, p. 18, my emphasis), he is certainly attaching a value to fiction as such, as he does to the perversity of a hysterical belief in what one knows to be imaginary: 'le lecteur peut dire sans cesse: *je sais bien que ce ne sont que des mots, mais tout de même...* (je m'émeus comme si ces mots énonçaient une réalité)' (p. 76).

5   'Au lieu de s'imposer comme péripéties dont le texte ne serait que l'effet, la fiction se déclare donc ici comme un effet de texte. Évitant de se confondre avec toute substance hallucinogène, le texte exige et définit la lecture qui déchiffrera son travail' (1971, p. 47). The opening pages of Marian Hobson's *The Object of Art* consider the conceptual implications of what she calls 'the present ill-repute of illusion' (1982, p. 3): 'What was Marxist in Berlin has become metaphysical in Paris: the *nouvelle critique* has striven to expel or restrict illusion, stigmatised as part of the "metaphysics of presence" in Western thought. For the weak

consumer of art it is a womb-like version of the search for the unmediated intuitive presence held rightly to be characteristic of some European philosophy [...] Thus, in certain modern criticism, one may find that illusion or surrogate concepts are expelled as undesirable aliens from modern writing: but the act of expulsion fails to take into account the dialectic between representation and form, between imaginative tissue and awareness of production. The failure is the more grave in that this dialectic forms the basis of the theory motivating the exclusion' (pp. 3–5).

6 See the whole of Barthes's essay 'Le mythe, aujourd'hui' (1957, pp. 191– 247), but especially pp. 195–213 for explanations of myth as a semiological system, and for the analysis of the *Paris Match* cover.

7 One might recall Sartre's analysis of the activity of 'imagining' (see chapter 1), where he claims that there is no possibility of analysing the details of the image, *since what is at stake is a matter of belief.*

REFERENCES

Auerbach, Erich, 1973. *Mimesis: the Representation of Reality in Western Literature*, translated by W. R. Trask (Princeton, Princeton University Press).

Barnes, Hazel E., 1981. *Sartre and Flaubert* (Chicago and London, University of Chicago Press).

Barthes, Roland, 1957. *Mythologies* (Paris, Seuil).

1964. *Essais critiques* (Paris, Seuil).

1970. *S/Z* (Paris, Seuil).

1973. *Le plaisir du texte* (Paris, Seuil).

1975. *Roland Barthes par Roland Barthes* (Paris, Seuil).

1977. *Fragments d'un discours amoureux* (Paris, Seuil).

1980. *La chambre claire: Note sur la photographie* (Paris, Gallimard/Seuil).

1981. *Le grain de la voix: Entretiens 1962–1980* (Paris, Seuil).

Bem, Jeanne, 1975. La production du sens chez Flaubert: la contribution de Sartre, in Gothot-Mersch, 1975, pp. 155–74.

1979. *Désir et savoir dans l'œuvre de Flaubert. Étude de 'La Tentation de Saint Antoine'* (Neuchâtel, Éditions de la Baconnière).

1981. *Clefs pour 'l'Éducation sentimentale'* (Tübingen, Naar, and Paris, Place).

Bernheimer, Charles, 1974. Linguistic realism in Flaubert's *Bouvard et Pécuchet*, *Novel* 7, pp. 143–58.

Bersani, Leo, 1968. The anxious imagination, *Partisan Review*, 35, pp. 49–66.

1974. Flaubert and Emma Bovary: the hazards of literary fusion, *Novel* 8, pp. 16–28.

Biasi, Pierre-Marc de, 1980. L'élaboration du problématique dans *La Légende de saint Julien l'Hospitalier*, in Debray-Genette, 1980, pp. 69–102.

Bosquet, Amélie, 1965. In *Les Amis de Flaubert* 26, p. 22.

Brombert, Victor, 1966. *The Novels of Flaubert: a Study of Themes and Techniques* (Princeton, Princeton University Press).

1971. *Flaubert par lui-même* (Paris, Seuil).

1975. *L'Éducation sentimentale*: articulations et polyvalence, in Gothot-Mersch, 1975, pp. 55–69.

Bruneau, Jean, 1962. *Les Débuts littéraires de Gustave Flaubert, 1831–1845* (Paris, Armand Colin).

References

Chambers, Ross, 1981. Simplicité de cœur et duplicité textuelle. Étude d'*Un Cœur simple*, *Modern Language Notes* 96, pp. 771–91.

Crouzet, Michel, 1969. Le style épique dans *Madame Bovary*, *Europe* 485–7, pp. 151–72.

Culler, Jonathan, 1974. *Flaubert: the Uses of Uncertainty* (London, Elek).

1975. *Structuralist Poetics: Structuralism, Linguistics and the Study of Literature* (London, Routledge and Kegan Paul).

1981. Une marge, in Dominique-Gilberte Laporte (ed.), *B et P centenaires* (Paris, La Bibliothèque d'Ornicar?), pp. 41–9.

Danger, Pierre, 1973. *Sensations et objets dans le roman de Flaubert* (Paris, Armand Colin).

Debray-Genette, Raymonde, 1970. Les figures du récit dans *Un Cœur simple*, *Poétique* 1, pp. 348–64.

1980 (ed.). *Flaubert à l'œuvre* (Paris, Flammarion).

1982. Description, dissection: *Par les Champs et par les grèves*, in P. M. Wetherill (ed.), *Flaubert: la dimension du texte* (Manchester, Manchester University Press), pp. 141–56.

Du Camp, Maxime, 1964. *Souvenirs littéraires 1822–1894* (extracts), in Flaubert, 1964, volume 1, pp. 19–37.

Felman, Shoshana, 1974. Illusion réaliste et répétition romanesque, *Change* 16–17, pp. 286–97.

1981. La signature de Flaubert: *La Légende de Saint Julien l'Hospitalier*, *Revue des sciences humaines* 181, pp. 39–57.

Flaubert, Gustave, 1926–30. *Correspondance*, 9 volumes (Paris, Conard).

1954. *Correspondance. Supplément*, 4 volumes (Paris, Conard).

1964. *Œuvres complètes*, edited by Bernard Masson, 2 volumes (Paris, Seuil).

1973. *Correspondance I (janvier 1830 à avril 1851)*, edited by Jean Bruneau (Paris, Gallimard).

1980. *Correspondance II (juillet 1851 à décembre 1858)*, edited by Jean Bruneau (Paris, Gallimard).

Forster, E. M., 1941. *Aspects of the Novel* (London, Edward Arnold).

Gaultier, Jules de, 1921. *Le Bovarysme* (Paris, Mercure de France).

Genette, Gérard, 1963. Le travail de Flaubert, *Tel Quel* 14, pp. 51–7.

1966(a). Frontières du récit, *Communications* 8, pp. 152–63.

1966(b). Silences de Flaubert, in *Figures* (Paris, Seuil), pp. 223–43.

1972. Discours du récit, in *Figures* III (Paris, Seuil), pp. 65–282.

Gervais, David, 1976. James's reading of *Madame Bovary*, *The Cambridge Quarterly* 7, pp. 1–26.

Gleize, Joëlle, 1974. Le défaut de ligne droite, *Littérature* 4, pp. 75–87.

Goethe, Johann Wolfgang von, 1962. *The Sorrows of Young Werther*, translated by Catherine Hutter (New York, New American Library).

Goncourt, Edmond and Jules de, 1956. *Mémoires de la vie littéraire 1851–1896*, 4 volumes (Paris, Fasquelle Flammarion).

Gothot-Mersch, Claudine, 1966. *La genèse de 'Madame Bovary'* (Paris, Corti).

References

1975 (ed.). *La production du sens chez Flaubert*. Colloque de Cerisy (Paris, Union générale d'éditions).

1979 (ed.). Gustave Flaubert, *'Bouvard et Pécuchet' avec un choix des scénarios, du Sottisier, l'Album de la Marquise et le Dictionnaire des idées reçues* (Paris, Gallimard).

Green, Anne, 1982. *Flaubert and the Historical Novel: 'Salammbô' Reassessed* (Cambridge, Cambridge University Press).

Hobson, Marian, 1982. *The Object of Art: the Theory of Illusion in Eighteenth-Century France* (Cambridge, Cambridge University Press).

Huss, Roger, 1977. Some anomalous uses of the imperfect and the status of action in Flaubert, *French Studies* 31, pp. 139–48.

James, Henry, 1962. Gustave Flaubert, in *The House of Fiction* (London, Mercury Books).

1981. *The Golden Bowl* (Harmondsworth, Penguin).

Jefferson, Ann, 1980. *The Nouveau Roman and the Poetics of Fiction* (Cambridge, Cambridge University Press).

Kawin, Bruce F., 1972. *Telling it Again and Again: Repetition in Literature and Film* (Ithaca and London, Cornell University Press).

Kierkegaard, Sóren, 1966. *The Concept of Irony: With Constant Reference to Socrates*, translated by Lee M. Capel (London, Collins).

Laing, R.D. and D.G. Cooper, 1971. *Reason and Violence: a Decade in Sartre's Philosophy* (London, Tavistock Publications).

Lapp, John C., 1956. Art and hallucination in Flaubert, *French Studies* 10, pp. 322–34.

Lawrence, D.H., 1955. Maestro Don Gesualdo, in *Selected Literary Criticism* (London, Heinemann), pp. 273–4.

Leavis, F.R., 1972. *The Great Tradition* (Harmondsworth, Penguin).

Lubbock, Percy, 1926. *The Craft of Fiction* (London, Cape).

Lukács, Georg, 1962. *The Historical Novel*, translated by Hannah and Stanley Mitchell (London, Merlin Press).

Mannoni, Octave, 1969. *Clefs pour l'Imaginaire ou l'Autre Scène* (Paris, Seuil).

Mouchard, Claude, and Jacques Neefs, 1980. Vers le second volume: *Bouvard et Pécuchet*, in Debray-Genette, 1980, pp. 169–217.

Neefs, Jacques, 1981. Descriptions de l'espace et espaces de socialité, in *Histoire et langage dans 'L'Éducation sentimentale' de Flaubert*, Colloque de la 'Société des études romantiques' (Paris, C.D.U./Sedes), pp. 111–22.

O'Connor, John R., 1980. Flaubert: *Trois Contes* and the figure of the double cone, *PMLA* 95, pp. 812–26.

Picard, Michel, 1973. La prodigalité d'Emma Bovary, *Littérature* 3, pp. 77–97.

Pommier, Jean, and Gabrielle Leleu (eds.), 1949. *'Madame Bovary'. Nouvelle Version précédée des scénarios inédits* (Paris, Corti).

Poulet, Georges, 1950. *Études sur le temps humain* (Paris, Plon).

References

Prendergast, Christopher, 1975. Flaubert: writing and negativity, *Novel* 8, pp. 197–213.

———1981. Flaubert: quotation, stupidity and the Cretan liar paradox, *French Studies* 35, pp. 261–77.

Proust, Marcel, 1927. A propos du style de Flaubert, in *Chroniques* (Paris, Gallimard).

———1954. *Du côté de chez Swann* (Paris, Gallimard).

Ricardou, Jean, 1967. *Problèmes du Nouveau Roman* (Paris, Seuil).

———1968. Fonction critique, in *Tel Quel, Théorie d'ensemble* (Paris, Seuil).

———1971. *Pour une théorie du Nouveau Roman* (Paris, Seuil).

Richard, Jean-Pierre, 1970. *Stendhal et Flaubert, 'Littérature et sensation'* (Paris, Seuil).

Rousset, Jean, 1962. *Forme et signification* (Paris, Corti).

Sarraute, Nathalie, 1966. Flaubert, *Partisan Review* 33, pp. 193–208.

Sartre, Jean-Paul, 1940. *L'Imaginaire; psychologie phénoménologique de l'imagination* (Paris, Gallimard).

———1960. *Questions de méthode* (Paris, Gallimard).

———1971–2. *L'Idiot de la famille. Gustave Flaubert de 1821 à 1857*, 3 volumes (Paris, Gallimard).

———1972. *Situations* IX (Paris, Gallimard).

———1976. *Situations* X (Paris, Gallimard).

Schor, Naomi, 1976. Pour une thématique restreinte: écriture, parole et différence dans *Madame Bovary, Littérature* 6, pp. 30–46.

Seed, D., 1979. Henry James' reading of Flaubert, *Comparative Literature Studies* 16, pp. 307–17.

Sherrington, R. J., 1970. *Three Novels by Flaubert. A study of techniques* (Oxford, Clarendon Press).

Tanner, Tony, 1979. *Adultery in the Novel: Contract and Transgression* (Baltimore and London, Johns Hopkins University Press).

Thibaudet, Albert, 1935. *Gustave Flaubert* (Paris, Gallimard).

Thorlby, Anthony, 1956. *Gustave Flaubert and the Art of Realism* (London, Bowes and Bowes).

Turnell, Martin, 1950. *The Novel in France* (London, Hamish Hamilton).

Valéry, Paul, 1960. *Œuvres* (Paris, Gallimard).

Warning, Rainer, 1982. Irony and the 'Order of Discourse' in Flaubert, *New Literary History* 13, pp. 253–86.

INDEX

Apuleius, *The Golden Ass*, 19
Artaud, Antonin, 46
Auerbach, Erich, 78, 113 n.10
Austen, Jane, 78

Balzac, Honoré de, 75, 85, 107–8
  n.2; *La Cousine Bette*, 26
Barnes, Hazel, 105 n.11
Barthes, Roland, 5, 15, 46, 86–7,
  89–90, 94, 99–102, 103 n.7,
  111 n.15, n.18, 114–15 n.19,
  116 n.1, 117 n.4, 118 n.6
Bem, Jeanne, 92–3, 105 n.11
Bernardin de Saint-Pierre,
  Jacques-Henri, *Paul et
  Virginie*, 63
Bernheimer, Charles, 43
Bersani, Leo, 111 n.16, 113–4 n.12
Biasi, Pierre-Marc de, 112 n.20
Bosquet, Amélie, 103 n.3
Brombert, Victor, 60, 105 n.11,
  n.17, 115 n.20
Bruneau, Jean, 112 n.2
Butor, Michel, *L'Emploi du
  temps*, 112 n.21

Cervantes, Miguel de, *Don
  Quixote*, 20
Chambers, Ross, 109 n.6
La Chanson de Roland, 58
Chateaubriand, François-René,
  La Vie de Rancé, 111 n.18
Colet, Louise, 36
Crouzet, Michel, 98
Culler, Jonathan, 4–5, 99, 103 n.5,
  105 n.11, n.14, 106 n.19,
  107 n.7, 113 n.7, 114 n.13,
  115 n.20, 117 n.3, n.4

Danger, Pierre, 110 n.13
Debray-Genette, Raymonde,
  110 n.8, 116–17 n.2
Derrida, Jacques, 116 n.1
Dickens, Charles, *Hard Times*,
  113 n.7
Diderot, Denis, 12
Du Camp, Maxime, 17, 19, 74

Felman, Shoshana, 72, 110 n.10
Flaubert, Gustave
  Bibliomanie, 26–7, 42, 75–6
  Bouvard et Pécuchet, 42–4, 45,
    53, 61, 68–9, 96–7, 98, 99,
    101, 102, 108 n.6, 111 n.18
  Un Cœur simple, 34, 38–40,
    41, 47, 51, 52, 57, 59, 61–5,
    77, 79, 99, 102, 107 n.7, n.8,
    109 n.6, n.7, 110 n.8, n.9,
    n.10, 113 n.11
  Correspondance, 10, 12, 13, 14,
    15–20, 21, 22, 25, 26, 34,
    36–7, 42, 45, 46, 54, 55, 59,
    75, 103 n.4, 104 n.3, n.4,
    105 n.12, n.15, 106 n.2,
    107 n.4, 108 n.5, 111 n.15,
    112 n.19
  L'Éducation sentimentale
    (1845), 26, 28–9, 45, 46, 47,
    49, 51–2, 53, 54, 60, 74–5,
    76, 90, 96, 102, 109 n.3,
    112 n.2, 113 n.6, 114 n.14
  L'Éducation sentimentale (1869),
    3–4, 34–7, 42, 46, 47–8,
    50–1, 52, 53, 57, 59, 60, 61,
    66, 70, 76, 85–93, 98, 99,
    103 n.4, 107 n.6, 109 n.4, 113
    n.4, n.8, 115 n.20, n.21, n.22

Index

Flaubert, Gustave (contd.)
   Hérodias, 46
   La Légende de Saint Julien
   l'Hospitalier, 39–40, 53, 66,
     70–3, 102, 112n.20, n.21,
     n.22, n.23
   Madame Bovary, 3, 26, 27, 28,
     29–34, 39, 41, 42, 44, 45,
     47, 49–50, 51, 52–3, 55–6,
     57, 58, 59, 61, 66–8, 70,
     76–85, 88, 89, 93–5, 98, 99,
     103–4n.7, 106n.2, 107n.3,
     n.5, 108n.3, 109n.1, n.5,
     110n.12, 113n.8, n.10, n.12,
     114n.15
   Mémoires d'un Fou, 45, 76,
     102, 106n.1, 114n.17
   Novembre, 14, 46, 53, 76,
     113n.5
   Par les Champs et par les
     grèves, 41, 97–8, 116–17n.2
   Un Parfum à sentir, 51
   Passion et vertu, 26, 27–8, 76
   Quidquid volueris, 26, 27, 74,
     75
   Rêve d'Enfer, 75
   Salammbô, 4, 20–4, 31, 48, 52,
     57, 76, 79, 99, 102, 105n.17,
     106n.18, n.19, 108n.3,
     110n.13, 113n.7, 115n.24
   Smarh, 75, 113n.3
   La Tentation de Saint Antoine,
     21, 75, 99, 113n.3
   Voyage en Orient, 7, 15–20,
     58, 115–16n.25
Forster, E.M., 3

Gaultier, Jules de, 82
Genette, Gérard, 41, 48, 56–7, 65,
   107–8n.2, 110n.11, 111n.17
Gervais, David, 104n.9
Gleize, Joëlle, 109n.4
Goethe, Johann Wolfgang von,
   20; *The Sorrows of Young*
   Werther, 75, 85, 86–7
Goncourt, Edmond and Jules de,
   21–2, 24
Gothot-Mersch, Claudine, 1–2,
   103n.2, 108n.4
Green, Anne, 105n.17

Hobson, Marian, 117n.5
Homer, 20, 75
Hugo, Victor, 26, 45
Huss, Roger, 65, 110n.14

James, Henry, 3–4, 5, 103n.4,
   104n.7, n.9
   The Golden Bowl, 5
   What Maisie Knew, 5
Jefferson, Ann, 103n.6

Kawin, Bruce F., 66
Kierkegaard, Søren, 97

Lacan, Jacques, 114n.19
Laing, R.D., 112n.1
Lamartine, Alphonse de, 26
Lapp, John C., 57
Lawrence, D.H., 3
Leavis, F.R., 1, 3, 103n.1
Lubbock, Percy, 114n.15
Lukács, Georg, 105n.17

Mannoni, Octave, 105n.8
Maupassant, Guy de, 34
Michelangelo, 20
Montesquieu, Charles de Secondat
   de, 45
Moore, George, 103n.1
Mouchard, Claude, 108n.4
Musset, Alfred de, 19

Neefs, Jacques, 108n.4, 114n.18

O'Connor, John R., 112n.23

Perruchot, Claude, 83
Picard, Michel, 111n.16, 113n.9
Plato, 111n.17
Poittevin, Alfred le, 42
Poulet, Georges, 57, 109n.2
Prendergast, Christopher, 109n.1,
   116n.1, 117n.4
Proust, Marcel, 65, 111n.16
   Un Amour de Swann, 90–1

Rabelais, François, 19, 20
Ricardou, Jean, 2, 4, 55, 69, 70,
   72, 99, 100, 112n.21, 117n.5
Richard, Jean-Pierre, 113n.8

Robbe-Grillet, Alain, *La Jalousie*, 57
Rousseau, Jean-Jacques, 111 n.18
   La Nouvelle Héloïse, 75, 85
Rousset, Jean, 115 n.23
Ruchiouk-Hânem, 15

Sainte-Beuve, Charles Augustin, 4
Sarraute, Nathalie, 110 n.13
Sartre, Jean-Paul, 7–15, 25–6, 41, 42, 74–5, 79, 86, 89, 90, 95, 104 n.5, n.6, 105 n.7, n.8, n.9, n.10, n.11, n.14, n.17, 108 n.6, 112 n.1, 114–15 n.19, 118 n.7
Schor, Naomi, 105 n.11
Seed, D., 104 n.8

Shakespeare, William, 20
   King Lear, 51
Sherrington, R. J., 76, 113 n.7
Sollers, Philippe, 46
Sophocles, *Oedipus Rex*, 70
Stendhal, 78
   Le Rouge et le Noir, 85

Taine, Hippolyte, 10
Tanner, Tony, 65, 110 n.12
Thibaudet, Albert, 105 n.17, 109 n.6, 111 n.16, n.18
Thorlby, Anthony, 85, 109–10 n.7
Turnell, Martin, 103 n.3, n.7

Valéry, Paul, 107 n.2

Warning, Rainer, 80